Doris Stokes is a celebrated clairaudient who
has confounded sceptics with the uncanny accuracy of
her readings. In Australia she filled the Sydney
Opera House and was mobbed in the streets; in this
country tickets are sold out for her
demonstrations within hours; she has appeared on the
Terry Wogan Show, and Desert Island Discs;
had a TV documentary devoted to her; been presented to
Princess Anne and receives hundreds of letters
from her huge following every week. In her books,
VOICES IN MY EAR, MORE VOICES IN MY
EAR, INNOCENT VOICES IN MY EAR, A HOST OF
VOICES and WHISPERING VOICES, she
describes how she discovered her extraordinary gift and
how she shares it with the world.
VOICES OF LOVE brings her remarkable story
up to date.

She lives in London with her husband John
and their son Terry.

11063 4969

DORIS STOKES
(with Linda Dearsley)

Voices of Love

Futura

A Futura Book

Copyright © Doris Fisher Stokes 1986

First published in Great Britain in 1986
by Futura Publications, a Division of
Macdonald & Co (Publishers) Ltd
London & Sydney

All rights reserved
No part of this publication may be reproduced,
stored in a retrieval system, or transmitted, in any
form or by any means without the prior
permission in writing of the publisher, nor be
otherwise circulated in any form of binding or
cover other than that in which it is published and
without a similar condition including this
condition being imposed on the subsequent
purchaser.

ISBN 0 7088 3125 7

Typeset by Leaper & Gard Ltd, Bristol, England
Reproduced, printed and bound in Great Britain by
Hazell Watson & Viney Limited,
Member of the BPCC Group,
Aylesbury, Bucks

Futura Publications
A Division of
Macdonald & Co (Publishers) Ltd
Greater London House
Hampstead Road
London NW1 7QX
A BPCC plc Company

'One day at a time, sweet Jesus'

Chapter One

I opened the *Daily Mirror* and there he was — on page three. Not a page three girl, but a sad little face peeping over a piece of sacking, one furry paw propping up his chin and a pair of mournful dark eyes staring out hopelessly. The message in those eyes was plain to read: I'm not really bad. Please won't somebody love me?

The pup had been named Boots after the scruffy mongrel in the *Mirror*'s popular strip cartoon, The Perishers, and he was desperate for a home.

Now I didn't intend to have a dog. Not me. Ever since we lost Matey, our ginger cat, I'd said never again. No more pets. We've had a succession of dogs and cats over the years and when Matey finally went out and failed to come home, I said enough's enough. The worry when they're ill, the anxiety when you go away, the sadness when they pass; I couldn't take it any more.

But Terry had other ideas. From the moment we'd moved into our new house he'd been pestering me about having a dog.

'When we've got all the building work done,' I kept

saying, playing for time because I've discovered that the extraordinary thing about having your own house is that it seems to mean one building job after another. No matter what you do there's always something else that needs attention. Sometimes I wonder why we don't just make up a bed for the builders and have done with it! They practically live here as it is.

Anyway it could be years before we'd finished with the builders at this rate, I thought, and by then Terry would have forgotten the idea.

So much for good intentions. One look at that poor little face in the *Daily Mirror* and I was lost. The puppy, a Jack Russell/dachshund cross, was only ten weeks old, yet he'd been abandoned twice in his short life. His second 'owner' had tired of him after two weeks and left him at Maidstone Police Station. The police sent him to an animal sanctuary but, said the paper, time was running out as they tried to find him a home.

Poor little soul, I thought looking at the bewildered face again, and that was it. Oh well, we'll manage somehow I sighed as I dialled directory enquiries for the number of Maidstone Police.

The police passed me on to the Viking Animal Sanctuary.

'Oh yes, the puppy in the *Daily Mirror*,' said the man who answered the phone. 'We've had two or three hundred calls about him. We'll be deciding in the next couple of days who he'll go to.'

Two or three hundred calls? We didn't stand much chance then, I thought as I gave the man my name and telephone number, and the funny thing was that although half an hour before I'd had no intention of having a dog, I was suddenly disappointed.

Never mind I told myself, at least that poor little

pup will get a good home, that's the main thing.

I put the paper away, got on with my work and pushed all thoughts of the dog firmly to the back of my mind.

'It's no good, Terry,' I said that evening as we were eating our tea. 'I've done everything I can but there were two or three hundred people after that dog.'

Terry was quite upset. He was still far from well, suffering from the affects of a head injury caused by an accident, and diabetes brought on by the shock. He'd obviously set his heart on this dog to cheer him up. I hadn't realised how much it meant to him. Oh dear, I thought as I cleared away the tea things, we'll have to go to Battersea Dogs Home or something and find him another one.

Then the next morning when I was in the middle of my huge pile of mail, the phone rang.

'It's for you, love,' said John.

'Mrs Stokes?' said a vaguely familiar voice. 'This is the Viking Animal Sanctuary. I just wanted you to know that we've decided to place Boots with you. That is if you still want him.'

'Oh yes. Yes of course we do,' I said, astonished. I'd completely given up hope of getting Boots.

'It was my wife that insisted,' the man went on. 'She's a fan of yours and as soon as she heard you'd phoned, that was it!'

I was delighted and Terry looked really cheerful for the first time in weeks. It was amazing to think that in twenty-four short hours, I'd gone from being adamant about never having another pet, to making arrangements to collect our new dog. I don't know, Doris, you ought to know better at your age, I told myself.

Tony Ortzen, our old friend and the editor of *Psychic News*, presented us with a large dog basket. Someone else gave us some old baby blankets, I got in a good supply of chicken pieces and we were all ready to collect the new arrival to the Stokes family.

Laurie, who as I explained in my last book, is friend, manager and general sounding board, drove us down to the Viking Animal Sanctuary. It was a friendly place, clean and efficiently run and while John and I chatted in the house over a cup of tea, one of the helpers went off to get Boots.

A few minutes later a tiny little scrap was put into my arms. Scarcely one foot long and weighing 5lbs, he was a warm, wriggling black and tan bundle, so full of affection and joy he didn't know whether to kiss my face, chew my fingers or dance round and round in my lap.

'Now Boots, keep still!' I laughed. 'Let's have a look at you.'

Two soft brown eyes, a pair of folded over black ears outlined faintly in gold, one white sock and a funny squiggly little tail that was currently going like a high speed windscreen wiper.

'Oh he's beautiful,' I cried. It was love at first sight.

The sanctuary gave us a little cage to take him home in. 'Use it whenever you take him out in the car,' they advised. And Boots was as good as gold, sitting perkily in the cage balanced on my lap.

Back home I found Terry slumped in an armchair watching television. He'd been feeling quite poorly that day. I didn't say anything. Quietly I opened the cage and put Boots on his lap. The change was dramatic. Within minutes Terry was laughing and pretending to protest as Boots clambered all over him licking his face, chewing his hair, chasing his slippers as if they were a pair of rats. From that moment on, Terry improved rapidly.

Within a very short time Boots ruled the house and I'm afraid to say he's spoiled rotten. All our good resolutions flew away within days.

'He stays downstairs in his basket at night,' I said. And so he did for about a week.

Then John and I went away for a couple of days and when we came back we found Boots wandering up to Terry's room at bedtime as if he owned the place. He'd got accustomed to sleeping with Terry and that was that.

'He stays in the cage when he goes out in the car,' I said. And so he did at first.

But then Terry opened the cage because he thought Boots was unhappy and from then on Boots had to sit on the passenger seat.

'He stays in the playpen in the garden while the builders are here,' I said. And so he did for ten minutes.

'Well he was crying you see, Mrs Stokes,' said one of the builders sheepishly, 'so we brought him out for a bit.'

It was hopeless but Boots is such a lovable little thing that you can't be cross with him. At first he chewed everything he could get his paws on. He chewed the carpet and my new rug, he chewed our slippers and any shoes left lying around, he chewed almost everything he could get his teeth into.

'Boots! No!' I yelled sometimes. 'I'll have your guts for garters!'

His only reply was to leap straight onto my knee and plant kisses all over my face as if I was speaking words of love. It was impossible to scold him.

Young as he was he seemed to have a long memory. I don't think he's ever forgotten the kindness shown to him at Maidstone police station, because he loves policemen. The first time Derek our local bobby dropped in, in uniform, for a cup of tea, Boots greeted him like a long lost friend. Now whenever Derek comes round he sits between his boots and looks up at him adoringly. And no matter how we spoil him I think there's still a lingering insecurity at the back of his mind. He's perfectly happy to go out for a walk but on the way back, the minute he sees the house he's off like the clappers and can't stop until he gets inside the gate. No matter what they say I'm sure that dogs and all animals have feelings. They knew where they're safe. They know where the love is.

These days of course Boots is quite a celebrity. I seem to do a lot of magazine and newspaper interviews and whenever there's an interviewer there's usually a photographer to go with him. As soon as Boots came along the photographers realised his potential and now he appears in just about every picture. Boots loves it. He's only got to see a camera and he automatically falls into an appealing pose, his ears prick up, his head tilts to one side and he arranges his paws neatly. Talk about star struck!

It was only a matter of time I suppose before Boots appeared on stage with me, but the night he made his debut it was just as much a surprise to me as it was to the audience.

We were at Birmingham Odeon one very hot day in September 1985. I always enjoy going to Birmingham because the people are so warm and friendly that they send out a tremendous wave of love to me on stage and it's an incredible help. The messages always flow faster when there's a good atmosphere.

Anyway this particular evening I finished the demonstration and was just about to move on to a little surprise I had for the audience, when the chairman suddenly sprang a surprise on me.

'Ladies and gentlemen, I've just had a note passed to me,' he said mysteriously. 'Will you please all welcome Doris' personal security.'

Personal security? I can't have heard that right, I thought, because although these days I have a manager, I certainly don't have any security, unless you count John of course. Puzzled, I glanced from the chairman to the audience, where a lot of tittering had started at the back.

To my amazement I saw an American cop, in full uniform with a gun on his hip and dark glasses covering his face, striding purposefully towards the stage. He was over 6 foot tall, as wide as a barn door, and he was holding something. I peered over the stage lights for a better view and when I saw what it was I began to laugh. This huge man was holding a long, extended lead and at the end of the lead was Boots, now grown to about 13 inches long and weighing about 6 lbs. The contrast between this enormous man and the tiny puppy was the funniest thing I'd ever seen and the audience were falling about.

Boots thought it was wonderful. As soon as he saw me he darted onto the stage, tying himself into knots and falling over his paws in his eagerness to reach me. The audience went wild and Boots played up to them outrageously. His tail wagged dementedly and he kissed everyone in sight. There was a terrific din of laughter and applause but it didn't worry him in the slightest. He took to it like a star.

Terry had planned the whole thing. While I thought he was safely at home looking after Boots, he was in fact tearing up the motorway to Birmingham. Throughout the evening he and Boots were hidden in a dressing-room upstairs, and Laurie's brother Alphi was persuaded to dress up in his American cop costume (don't ask me how he got it — I haven't the faintest idea) and lead Boots onto the stage.

Funnily enough, all evening I'd sensed that something was going on but I couldn't think what it could be. The spirit world didn't want to spoil the surprise by telling me the secret but there was no mistaking the feeling of anticipation in the air.

Alphi was so taken with Boots, in fact, that he wrote this lovely poem about him which sums him up perfectly!

Boots

Today I bit the postman
and then I chased the cat
Went into my mum's wardrobe
and chewed up her best hat
I tore up Daddy's slipper
and ate the morning post
Then jumped up on the table
and ate the breakfast toast.

I nearly caught a sparrow
As it landed in the yard
But now I am exhausted
Because I play so hard.

I think I'll have a little nap
Maybe I will snore
And then when I wake up
I will chase the boy next door.

Alphi O'Leary

That visit to Birmingham was very special for many reasons. Most of all I think because my first appearance (I did two) coincided with those terrible riots in Handsworth and at the end of the evening we had to warn people not to travel home through that part of the city. Yet while all that violence and destruction was going on just a mile or two up the road, hundreds of people were generating so much love and warmth and compassion for each other. It just shows the two extremes we're capable of.

When we arrived at the stage door that night we found three ladies standing outside, drenched in tears.

'Oh Doris, can we just give you this letter,' sobbed one of them. 'We wanted to make sure you'd read it. We've left one at the front door too, just in case we didn't see you.'

Laurie quickly took the letter from my hand.

'I'm sorry, ladies,' he said, 'Doris can't stay now, she mustn't be seen talking to anyone, but I'll come back and speak to you in a minute.' And he hurried me inside.

'Oh Laurie,' I said, 'they obviously need help desperately.'

'I know, love, I'll sort something out, but you know what it's like.'

Laurie can be a worrier at times but I understood his concern. The more well-known you get, the more people there are just dying to criticise and if I stood chatting at the stage door with members of the audience before a show I'd be accused of cheating. It's the same with the letters. Quite often people will send letters to the theatre where I'm appearing, appealing for me to contact their loved ones during the evening. I couldn't read them even if I wanted to, it would be called collusion. Instead I hand them, still sealed, either to Laurie or the chairman and I don't look at them until I get home.

Naturally I couldn't read this particular letter but the sight of those distressed ladies worried me.

'We're all right now, Laurie,' I said as soon as John and I were settled in the dressing-room. 'See if you can have a word with those ladies.'

They were still there at the stage door. Laurie explained as gently as he could why I couldn't read their letter until after the show but he promised that I would see it eventually.

'Are you going to the demonstration?' he asked.

They shook their heads. 'No, the tickets were sold out ages ago. We only came to deliver the letter.'

'Well would you like to go?' Good old Laurie often keeps back one or two tickets for special emergencies.

The ladies were thrown into confusion. They obviously hadn't come hoping for preferential treatment.

'We haven't got ourselves ready to go in!' they protested.

'How ready d'you have to be!' laughed Laurie. 'You look all right to me.'

That did it. They all accepted the tickets and in a much more cheerful frame of mind they hurried round to the front of the house to find their seats.

I'd known from the moment I'd set eyes on those ladies that it was important I should speak to them and the spirit world was clearly organising the whole thing.

Later during the demonstration a determined Brummie voice said in my ear, 'I'm Ellen but everyone calls me Nelly, and I'm looking for Pat.'

'I've got an Ellen called Nelly looking for Pat,' I repeated out loud. 'Is Pat here?'

Immediately a middle-aged woman came hurrying down to the microphone. There was something a bit familiar about her but I didn't twig at first that it was the sobbing lady from the stage door.

'Nelly's my mother,' said Pat eagerly.

Even then I didn't take a good look at her because I was concentrating so hard on what Nelly was telling me. It was bad news and I'd have to phrase it very carefully.

'Well, love, your mother's telling me she's very concerned about Mary. She's in the hospital, isn't she?'

'Yes she is,' said Pat.

Nelly told me that they were preparing to fetch Mary very soon but I didn't like to come straight out with it.

'Mary's *very* poorly. You know that, don't you,' I began tactfully.

'Oh yes Doris, we know she's dying,' said Pat and as she drew out her handkerchief to dab her eyes I recognised her. 'She was so disappointed not to be able to come tonight,' Pat went on. 'She's always been to see you when you've been at the Odeon. She hasn't missed one show.'

'She's only young,' put in Nelly sadly and as she said it I felt a terrible pain around my liver. I recognised the signs.

'The poor child. It's your sister, isn't it?' I said. 'Is it in the liver?'

Pat confirmed that her sister was indeed suffering from cancer of the liver.

'Well look love, never mind about her not coming tonight. If I can find the time tomorrow I'll go and see her in the hospital to make up for it!'

Pat was a bit astonished, I think, but she left her sister's full name and the address of the hospital with Laurie and at the end of the evening when I was presented with a beautiful bouquet of flowers I held them up for Pat to see.

'Where are you, Pat?' I called out into row upon row

17

of faces. I had no idea where she was sitting but it didn't matter. 'I'll take this bouquet to Mary.'

The next day I was recording a programme for Ed Doolan on BBC radio and there was another demonstration at the Odeon in the evening, but there was just enough time between the two for a visit to Selly Oak Hospital.

Unfortunately it wasn't visiting time but a nurse came out of the ward to speak to us.

'Is it possible to see Mary Woodley?' I asked. 'I promised her mother I'd come and see her but I'm so busy this was the only moment free. I've got a theatre appearance tonight you see.'

I didn't even attempt to explain that Mary's mother was on the other side when I'd made my promise. I felt that could complicate things immensely.

'Just one moment,' said the nurse, 'I'll ask sister.'

A few moments later she was back, 'Yes that's all right but you mustn't stay too long.'

Clutching the huge bouquet, I was shown into a beautiful ward. Long and airy with huge windows pouring sunshine into the room, it was in no way a gloomy miserable place.

Mary was at the far end and she wasn't expecting me, yet she heard my voice, recognised it immediately and tried to get off the bed. Sadly she was too weak but the sister saw her struggle and hurried forward.

'It's all right, sister,' I said, 'I won't stay long. I just want to give her a message.'

Poor Mary was only thirty-five and she was such a smart girl even in bed. She'd gone very thin and her skin was sallow with the illness but she was wearing a pretty nightdress and she'd had her hair cut stylishly.

'Doris!' she cried as I sat on the bed. 'I knew that was your voice but I didn't believe it!'

18

She was a brave girl. She admired the flowers and chatted brightly even though she was probably in pain. Nelly arrived within minutes.

'Your mum's here, Mary love,' I said. 'She's never far away from you.'

'Tell her not to be afraid, Doris,' said Nelly. 'It won't be long now and I'll be there to take her hand.'

Mary's face lit up when I gave her this message.

'There's nothing to it, love,' I went on, 'there's nothing to be afraid of. Your mother'll be with you every step of the way.'

By the time we left I truly believe that Mary's fears had been eased. Her face had a great peacefulness about it and I knew that it had been worth every minute of my afternoon off to bring a little comfort to a very special girl. If I achieved nothing else in Birmingham, that visit to Mary made the whole trip worthwhile.

Afterwards I received a lovely letter from Pat telling me that the message from Nelly was the best medicine Mary could have had and that she was a changed girl since the visit.

But if I thought I could rest on my laurels in the remaining couple of hours before the evening's show, the spirit world had other ideas.

Our terrible summer had turned into a beautiful autumn and the centre of Birmingham was stifling. We opened all the windows in our hotel room but somehow we couldn't seem to catch a whiff of a breeze.

'Come on, love, put your feet up and rest,' John kept urging me, but I couldn't. Two young spirit boys were plaguing me, in the nicest possible sense of course.

One of them, a poor, mixed-up lad before he passed, told me he'd shot himself in the head and whenever he came close I got a searing pain through my temples. He was so unused to communicating that he didn't know how to talk to me without flooding me with his last impressions.

'I'm sorry, Doris,' he said, 'but I'm going to get through tonight even if I give you a blinding headache. I must tell Mum I'm sorry.'

No sooner had he moved away than another boy was mentally tugging at my sleeve.

'It's Paul,' he said. 'You won't forget, will you?'

Paul was rather forlorn because he'd come through the night before at the Odeon and the young woman over whose head his light was hovering refused to acknowledge him. I discovered later that she was related in some way to Paul but she was either too shy or too bewildered to come forward so Paul's messages were wasted. But Paul wouldn't give up.

'You will try again tonight, won't you?' he kept asking. 'They'll be there tonight. You won't forget?'

'I'll do my best, love,' I promised, 'but if they don't turn up or they won't answer, what can I do?'

Paul wandered away but every half hour or so his voice drifted back ... 'Don't forget ...'

I'm not likely to with you pair around all the time, I grumbled to myself as I abandoned all hope of having a nap and changed into my long dress for the stage. But I wasn't really cross, and besides this was to be a special evening.

For some time now I'd been supporting a charity called PHAB which stands for Physically Handicapped and Able Bodied. It's an organisation in which the physically handicapped and able bodied mix together socially; the able bodied to help the handicapped and the handicapped to enrich the lives of the able bodied. As well as social evenings PHAB likes to organise outings for its members but they were always in need of new minibuses fitted with wheelchair lifts to carry the handicapped.

Now as I've said before, my old dad always used to tell me: 'Cast your bread upon the waters, Dol, and it will come back buttered' and I've tried to carry out his words ever since. Every year I do as much work as I can for charity and in the past I've simply handed over the cheque to whichever charity I'm supporting, and that's the end of it. Wouldn't it be nice if for a change I could actually see what the money had paid for? I thought. If I gave something they really needed instead. And that's how the idea for the bus arose.

It took a while to raise the necessary £15,000, but at last we got the money together, ordered the bus and made arrangements to hand it over at Birmingham on September 11th. Unfortunately in the end the bus we'd chosen wasn't ready in time; it was still being fitted with the special lifts and painted pale blue, the healing colour, with the words 'The Spirit of Love' on the side. So instead, the company lent us an identical bus to present on the night.

There were quite a few PHAB members in the audience that night and the presentation was to be a surprise for them, but Paul nearly gave the game away in the very first message.

'Now I must start with a message I got last night,' I explained to the audience. 'This Paul Wilson or Wilcox came through and gave me a lot of names but his people weren't there to accept them and he's been on at me all afternoon to try again tonight. He tells me he was in a wheelchair and the address Shepherds Road is important. I do hope someone's here tonight for him.'

This time Paul was in luck. Almost at once a bright, bubbly young girl came down to the microphone.

'It's Paul Wilkins,' she said, 'and I'm Paul's oldest sister.'

Paul, who'd arrived the minute I set foot on stage, breathed a sigh of relief.

'That's Carole spelled with an "e",' he said happily.

He was clearly very fond of Carole.

'Are you Carole with an "e"?' I asked.

'Yes,' she said grinning, 'and I live in Shepherds Road.'

I knew we were spot on now and Carole didn't seem a bit nervous which helped things along nicely. What's more, Paul was getting quite good at communicating now, having practised the night before, and the evidence came pouring through.

'He's giving me a name which sounds like Suliman,' I said.

'That's right, my married name's Suliman,' said Carole.

'And someone called Rashid, I think that was.'

'My husband.'

Paul evidently approved of Rashid. 'He's a good bloke,' he said.

Carole giggled when I passed this on. 'Yes he is.'

Paul went on to explain a bit about himself. He was only twenty-seven when he passed, a physically handicapped boy who sometimes got frustrated and irritated because he couldn't do all the things he wanted to do.

'At times I used to cry because I felt so useless,' he said. 'But then I joined PHAB and it helped me help others. I'm glad I did something worthwhile.'

If you've got to go there can't be a better way than the way Paul passed. 'It was very quick,' he said 'I went to bed, Mum kissed me goodnight, I said "I love you, Mum" and then I went to sleep and woke up over here. That's the way to do it.'

After he passed he said his mother cut off a lock of his hair. Mrs Wilkins, who'd shyly come forward to join her daughter at the microphone, confirmed that this was true.

'I'm going to put it in a locket,' she said.

Paul went on to mention his stepfather Alan, his uncle Brian and the fact that he'd left £42.16 in his wallet. Then he started muttering something about a tea caddy or teapot and I couldn't make it out at all.

'I think he's saying something about a tea caddy,' I told Carole. 'I don't know what he means. Why's he telling me that?'

Carole's hand flew to her mouth in amazement.

'Oh,' she gasped, 'I thought I was imagining that. I keep my keys in the teapot in the kitchen and just lately when there's no-one around, they've been rattling. I thought it must be my imagination.'

'No, it was Paul,' I assured her. 'He's trying to tell you he's there.'

Paul gave one or two more details, then he mentioned someone called Barr. I had no idea as I passed this name on that Paul was naughtily hinting about the special surprise.

'Mr Barr. Oh that's the man who drives the handicapped bus,' said Paul's mother.

Paul chuckled wickedly, 'And I hope he'll be the first to have the pleasure of driving the new one.'

'Paul! You're giving secrets away,' I scolded.

'He says he hopes he'll be the first to have the pleasure,' I paraphrased, 'and only we know what he means.'

Paul got the evening off to a good start and when he finally moved away to let the other spirit people have a turn the messages came rushing along. The boy who'd

23

shot himself explained that he didn't know what came over him. He was moody and depressed and believed that no-one understood how he felt.

'I finally got a job and I was only there a week when they kicked me out,' he said, 'so I thought bugger it.'

He mentioned some family names and his friends Stephen and Peter, particularly Peter. 'I wish I'd talked to Peter,' he said. 'He would have stopped me.'

There was six-year-old Claire, the image of her daddy.

'There's my daddy Martin,' she cried as her parents came to the microphone. Claire was perfectly happy in her new life, only one thing bothered her.

'I never got to unpack my presents from you,' she said, still annoyed because she'd passed just before Christmas.

Then there was Gary, the boy who'd been killed giving some friends a lift home; a little toddler who'd drowned in a swimming pool; a husband who knew that his wife had had her kitchen remodelled since he passed and that there wasn't room in it for her washing machine; and so on and so on. Back they all came, husbands and wives, fathers and mothers, sisters, brothers and little children ... until at last I had to rest and it was time to make the presentation.

The mini bus was already on the stage, hidden from the audience by a thick curtain, and Ed Doolan from Pebble Mill came to the theatre specially to make the announcement.

He talked a little bit about PHAB, then two members of the group came onto the stage: Hayley a little blind girl with two stumps instead of legs, was pushed on in a wheelchair by her helper Scott. She couldn't see and she couldn't walk, but she had beautiful skin, dark glossy hair and the sweetest smile. She presented me with a bouquet of flowers and that, she thought, was the end of it. But I knew better.

'Do you enjoy going to the PHAB club, Hayley?' I asked.

'Oh yes. I live for club evenings.'

'And what d'you think your club would like most in all the world?'

Hayley thought for a moment. 'Well ... we need a new mini bus because ours keeps breaking down,' she said.

So I opened her hand and put the keys in her palm.

Puzzled, she felt the cold metal. 'What are these?'

'They're the keys for your new bus, darling,' I told her. 'Here it is.'

And the curtain rose and there was the bus in all it's splendour. But Hayley of course couldn't see it, so we pushed her up close so that she could feel it instead. Silently she ran her hands over the sparkling paintwork.

'Oh isn't it shiny, Scott,' she whispered.

'Yes,' he said, 'that's because it's brand new.'

The look on their faces was the best reward I could have hoped for. I can't describe the feeling I got that night. People keep saying to me, 'Why on earth are you spending all this money?' But what's the point of being the richest body in the cemetery? If I can make those kids happy it makes me happy too and whenever I think of them enjoying their bus in the years to come I get a warm glow.

A wealthy friend of mine was going on at me about it just the other day. She had recently separated from her rich husband who had spent his health to gain his wealth and was currently trying to spend his wealth to buy back his health. This lady stood there in her mink coat, with her Mercedes sports car parked outside and her large house all paid for out of her husband's company, and between scolding me about giving my money away she complained bitterly about the pittance her mean husband gave her to live on.

'D'you know I'm supposed to manage on £19.50 a day,' she moaned.

'For goodness sake listen to yourself,' I said, losing patience. 'You're talking exactly like your husband. You've been with him so long you think like him. Stop counting how much this cost and how much that cost. Would you rather be miserable with a millionaire or have your self respect and make do? And as for my money, I'd much rather see it being used by some child that needs it than locked up in a bank.'

There was a stunned silence. I hope she wasn't offended but I couldn't help coming out with it.

There was a postscript to my Birmingham visit. A few weeks after we returned home I was arranging some flowers in front of the photographs of my spirit children, when suddenly I saw the face of Mary, the girl I'd visited in Selly Oak Hospital. I only caught a tiny glimpse of her but her complexion was a warm rosy colour and her face was shining with health.

'I'm safe with Mum now, Doris,' she said.

And Nelly's voice chimed in, 'Will you tell our Pat?'

Laurie was dropping in that day and I knew he had Pat's number somewhere in his office so I asked him to pass the message on. Sure enough, when he phoned, he discovered that Mary had just passed over.

But even that wasn't the end of the story. A few months and many many communications later we were invited back to the Odeon at Birmingham and Pat was in the audience once more. There were hundreds of other people present of course and the messages were flying in all directions so when Nelly and Mary came back yet again I didn't recognise them at first. But then Mary said, 'You came to see me in hospital you know,' and it all fell into place.

'Tell Pat I'd had enough,' said Mary. 'I got so weak and sick I kept saying, "Come on Mum, take my hand." And one day I went to sleep and Mum came and took me home. I wasn't sorry. I'd had enough.' She went on to tell me that Pat had got her ring but that most of her other things were still just as she'd left them.

'I don't know why, because I'm not going to come back and use them,' said Mary. She was particularly concerned about her new red sweater. She was very fond of it and didn't want it given away. She wanted someone in the family to wear it.

She also talked of her husband. 'He was a good husband in one way,' said Mary, 'but we couldn't live together. We parted, so in the end all I had was my family but they are a wonderful family. When I took the final step there were four of them round my bed.'

Most of all I think she was concerned about Pat.

'She's under a lot of stress at the moment and things are difficult at home. She's worrying she's going to get cancer like me. Tell her not to worry and not to be a doormat.'

Finally Mary wanted Pat to know that she was healthy and fit once more. 'Remember the last time you saw me, how I looked?' she asked.

'Yes,' said Pat, 'terrible.'

'Well I'm not like that any more. Forget it. I'm back to normal.'

By the end of the evening Pat was smiling and cheerful.

'I'm a different person now,' she wrote to me afterwards, 'I no longer feel sad and downhearted, and strange as it might sound I feel happy for Mary.'

Yes, all in all, when I look back on my visits to Birmingham, I think I can safely say it was time well spent.

Chapter Two

The girl was young and pretty with long red-brown hair falling over her shoulders and she was sobbing her heart out. She sat hunched up on the back stairs at the SAGB (the headquarters of the Spiritualist Association of Great Britain) crying as if the end of the world had come, and not caring a bit who saw her.

My friend Nancy and I had just stepped out of the lift on our way back from a quick sandwich lunch and we stopped dead.

'Whatever's the matter, love,' I asked gently.

'I've just lost a very good friend,' she gulped between sobs, 'and I can't get into the demonstration. It's full.' And the tears started falling again.

'Come on, love,' said Nancy, 'we'll get you in if you have to sit on the floor.'

It was one of those days. I don't often get the chance to do a full day at SAGB and when I do it's usually packed out. I'd had to leave home before 10.00 that morning for the first session and there was only time for a quick bite and a cup of tea before I had to start all over again. They'd got them wedged like sardines in that hall and the central heating was going full blast despite the fact that it was a mild day. It was like stepping into a turkish bath.

Nancy had a word with the man on the door and a box was pushed in beside the grand piano for the young girl. It didn't look very comfortable but it was the best we could do.

I started to work normally and then to my surprise a faint light flew directly over the girl's bright hair and a young male voice said, 'I was found dead in bed yesterday.'

Yesterday, I thought, no wonder the poor girl's in such a state.

'I've got a young man here who was found dead in bed yesterday,' I told her. 'Does that mean anything to you, love?'

'Yes!' she cried and burst into tears again.

The young man tried to tell me his name but it was difficult for him to communicate so soon after passing and I could hardly hear him.

'Was that Gary, love?' I asked.

'Yes,' said the girl, 'his name's Gary.'

He was trying to give me his surname too but I couldn't catch it. It was something like Alton or Almon.

'No I don't think I've got that right,' I said to him, 'try me again Gary.'

To my surprise he laughed and started whistling instead. What on earth's going on I thought? If I can't make out what he's saying, how's whistling going to help? Then I realised that the tune sounded familiar. It was like a pop song, yet it wasn't a pop song because I'm not very good at those and I knew this tune well. Then I realised where I'd heard it before. It was the theme tune of one of my favourite TV programmes, *Auf Wiedersehen Pet*.

'It can't be,' I said out loud in shock. 'Surely it can't be Gary Holton from *Auf Wiedersehen Pet*?'

'Yes it is,' said Gary and his friend simultaneously.

Gary Holton was the talented young man who played a popular cockney character called Wayne in the TV series. His sudden death the day before had been all over the morning papers but I'd left too early to see them and I'd known nothing about it. The episode really shook me. I come across tragedy all the time in my job of course but to have someone you watch every week on TV turn up suddenly amongst the spirit voices when you didn't even know they'd passed, is quite a shock.

Gary went on to mention a few more names but the girl was so distressed I felt it would be kinder to move on to another contact. Making a mental note to have a word with her at the end, I continued with the demonstration. It passed smoothly enough with no more unpleasant shocks. Afterwards I collected up my things and looked around for the young girl, but she'd gone.

'Oh she left you this,' said the man on the door handing me a slip of paper.

It was a hasty note thanking me for my help and signed Melanie — no address, no telephone number. Oh well, never mind, I thought, that's the end of that and I went home, sad that we'd lost a bright young talent but certain that I'd heard the last of the affair.

Which just shows how wrong you can be even when you're a medium!

Gary Holton was quite determined to come back for a long chat because unknown to me, he'd made an unofficial appointment three weeks before he passed and he still intended to keep it even though he was now on the other side!

It happened like this. A friend of mine met Gary Holton and his girlfriend Jahnette in Marbella, Spain, where the *Auf Wiedersehen Pet* team were filming the Spanish scenes for the series. Over drinks in the hotel bar my name was mentioned and Gary and Jahnette said how much they'd like to meet me. The upshot was that my friend agreed to bring them over for a cup of tea on my first day off after Gary had finished filming. No one could have guessed then that Gary Holton, apparently fit, healthy and full of life, had only three short weeks left on this earth.

The TV crew stayed on for an extra week or two, then they returned to Nottingham to shoot the final scenes. It was a hectic schedule for them because they were up against a deadline and every minute counted. Everyone was working very hard indeed but Gary didn't seem to be showing any more strain than anyone else. On the Thursday afternoon he finished his work in the Nottingham studios and set off for London to be ready for the read through at the rehearsal rooms the next morning. He never got there. On Friday morning Jahnette found him dead in bed.

Yet Gary obviously hadn't forgotten that planned meeting with me and I believe that one of the first things he did when he found himself over there, was to set about organising it.

First he prompted Melanie, a young actress he'd worked with who knew a lot about spiritualism, to come to the SAGB at short notice despite the fact that there were no places left. Then he made sure that Nancy and I were returning from lunch at just the right moment to bump into her and he also made sure that he got a message through. He's clearly a very determined young man when he puts his mind to it.

Jahnette of course quickly got to hear of Melanie's

message, and remembering the discussion in Spain she was keen to keep the appointment.

She arrived one grey winter morning with her friends Brian and Susie. She was still suffering from shock. She was wrapped in a thick fur coat, the collar pulled up to her ears, yet she looked frozen, just the same.

'Come in and have a cup of tea, love,' I said, getting her quickly indoors and turning the fire up. Her friend Susie looked almost as cold. Only Brian seemed calm and unruffled.

Gary came through almost at once but it was difficult to keep up with him. His voice was instantly recognisable, that broad cockney accent and the language at times! Well it's a good thing I'm unshockable. But despite this, there was a great deal of confusion around him and at times his voice was so faint I could hardly hear a word he said.

At this time Jahnette was still waiting for the outcome of the inquest and we didn't know the official cause of death, although the papers were full of speculation.

Shortly before the tragedy it was revealed that Gary had been a heroin addict and of course now everyone was saying that it was a drug overdose which killed him.

Gary was very annoyed about this.

'I didn't do it. It wasn't drugs,' he insisted. 'I'd kicked heroin. Don't let them say that.'

Then great waves of confusion would come flowing in, he didn't seem to know how he'd ended up on the other side. It had been a great surprise to him at first.

'I was very angry, very bitter when I realised what had happened,' he said, his voice getting agitated again. 'I was just making it. Finally I was making it and then this had to happen. It's not fair.'

'Don't upset yourself, love,' I said gently. 'Tell me about something else.'

'It's okay, I'm at peace now,' he said calming down, but he changed the subject all the same. He mentioned the names John and Tony.

'John's his manager and Tony is a reporter who's writing about him at the moment,' said Jahnette. 'And now he's talking about Amanda and Lisa,' I explained.

'They're girlfriends of his,' said Jahnette who didn't seem at all bothered or jealous of them.

'I borrowed a tenner from Brian before it happened,' Gary went on. 'Sorry mate, you won't get that back.'

Brian smiled ruefully. He clearly didn't begrudge Gary the money.

But talk of events leading up to the tragedy set Gary reassessing his life again.

'Five years. I wasted so much time ... I was f. ...' I hastily censored the last word.

He went on to talk of his wife Donna and his long time girlfriend Susie and predicted that there would be a lot of confusion and nastiness over the funeral.

'But I had good friends in Brian and Jahnette,' he added. 'We understood each other, we could tell what each other was thinking. There was nothing we couldn't talk about.'

But he was slipping into sadness again. 'I lived my life and made a mess of it ...'

'All right, love, don't go on about it,' I said. 'What's been happening lately?'

At first I didn't think he was paying attention but after a second or two, very faintly, I heard something about a house in the country, near Little something. There was the hiss of an 's' sound but that's all I could make out.

'It must be Little Saxham,' said Jahnette. 'We went to look at a house out that way because we wanted to open a centre to help heroin addicts.'

'That's what's going to happen,' said Gary determinedly. 'With Pip. I'll still help you. Just put out your hand and I'll be there.'

Then he started to laugh. 'I'm thirty-three you know but the papers said thirty-two. Don't take any notice of the bloody papers. You can't believe a word they say. And never mind what they said about Brian and Jahnette. The happiest time of my life I have them to thank for. They're true blue. We loved each other. I had a lot of girls on the side but we understood each other.'

He was still very concerned about his friends.

'You've been a very mixed up little girl,' he told Jahnette, 'but now you're beginning to get yourself together. The tears you've shed. We've cried in each others arms, talking about wouldn't it be better if we went. Promise me you'll learn something from this. Do something positive.'

And as for Brian he was worried that he wasn't making the most of his talent.

'Brian's the sort of bloke who gives up if things don't go right,' he said. 'Lazy bugger. He has so much talent but he doesn't use it. He can write. I love Brian as a soul mate and I don't want him to fritter his life away. He's got lyrics in the drawer that have never been used. Get on with it mate and I'll help you.'

By now Gary was wandering back and forth between the two of them.

'That girl held me in her arms and I sweated and shook,' he said, 'but I'd sorted myself out and then this had to happen. It's not f ... fair. I would have shown them. I frittered away a lot of money but I was also screwed out of a lot of money. I trusted people. I had no business head.'

After his passing, the papers had been full of terrible stories about Gary and he was particularly upset about one report which linked him with an 11-year-old girl.

'I had three children. I wouldn't have touched an 11-year-old, I've got three kids of my own. Oh I'm well off out of it,' he finished angrily.

This puzzled me because I could have sworn I'd read somewhere that Gary had only one child, but Jahnette explained.

'Yes I know what he means. He's talking about Max, Susie's son from a past marriage, and Danielle my daughter as well as his own son. He loved them and thought of them as his own children. He would say he's got three kids.'

'I always supported the baby,' Gary went on, 'but Brian listen, I have creditors. I owe money. My kid won't get anything unless we're careful.'

By now the power was fading badly and it was a strain to make out his words, but still Gary went on, remembering his friends.

'Amanda. She's only nineteen. Give her my love. I was a bit of a sod but I loved her. There's one thing, Jahnette. They said they loved me and I wondered if it was because I was famous but I never thought that about Jahnette. She loved me for me, warts and all. I took advantage of all those others. But then who wouldn't?'

He talked of his friends Steve and Melanie and finally of Ben.

'Oh I'm glad he's mentioned Ben,' said Jahnette. 'Ben's Keith Moon's son and Gary helped him through a very difficult time in his life. He thought the world of Ben.'

36

But Gary was gone and I was exhausted. Yet the sitting wasn't quite over. Jahnette's friend Susie had been sitting quietly curled up in an armchair throughout the conversation. The poor girl seemed very subdued and it wasn't until Gary had finished that she shyly mentioned that one or two of the names Jahnette hadn't been able to place might have been intended for her. It turned out that young as she was, she had been recently widowed and she was still suffering badly.

I couldn't let her leave without some word of comfort, so I tuned in once more, gathering up the last shreds of power. Fortunately it wasn't a struggle. Her husband John had been hovering close trying to get a word in throughout the sitting. In fact one puzzling comment I'd heard soon after they'd arrived now became clear.

In the middle of the confusion surrounding Gary, I made out the words, 'We parted on bad terms. I'm sorry. I forgive you,' and the words were spoken very definitely to Susie. There was no question of the message being intended for Jahnette or Brian.

Susie however was puzzled. 'No it can't be for me. I never met Gary,' she said.

No one present could understand it and we let it go but now I realised that it had been Susie's husband trying to interrupt right at the beginning. The story was particularly tragic because they'd parted company unhappily, the husband had gone abroad and been killed in a car accident.

'It was two days before I was due home,' he said. 'Just two days that's all.'

He talked of the accident, the sons he'd left behind and some of the problems of the marriage. It was only a mini sitting because by now I was exhausted, but it seemed to cheer Susie quite a bit.

Afterwards over a cup of tea, Jahnette explained a little more about poor Gary's mixed-up life. Apparently he'd had quite a wild time. He'd been a child actor, then a pop singer and he'd got involved in drink, drugs and goodness knows what else. Then came his unexpected success in the first series of *Auf Wiedersehen Pet* and instead of bringing him pleasure, it seemed only to create more problems. Work poured in and to cope with the work he leaned more heavily on drugs. His relationship with his girlfriend Sue, the mother of his son, began to suffer and soon he was in a pretty bad way.

Jahnette found him in her local pub in a distressed state as he tried to escape the unwelcome attentions of a group of fans. She took him home and soon he was more or less living with her and her steady boyfriend Brian. It might be a funny idea to an old lady like me, but it seems to have suited them. Gary had other girlfriends and Jahnette had Brian but the three of them lived together without jealousy.

'Gary managed to kick heroin,' said Jahnette, 'and he was really getting himself together. We had great plans. He was just starting to realise what he could achieve. He was very concerned about drugs and young people and he felt he could use his fame to do so much to help drug addicts because he'd been through it himself. He wanted to open a special centre in the country.

'The only problem was money. The way he'd been living he'd run into debt. He'd earned a lot of money but he'd spent even more, so he was working very hard to get straight. He'd come out of a year in a play which is very tiring in itself, straight into the second series of *Auf Wiedersehen Pet*. It was such a tight schedule and everybody had to work incredibly hard, but as soon as filming was over Gary was getting ready for a season in pantomime.'

The week before the tragedy was particularly unhappy. Sensational newspaper reports seemed to follow Gary wherever he went and that week his heroin addiction was revealed.

'He was very upset about it,' said Jahnette, 'he thought that no one would believe he was cured and that his career would be ruined. Then that last day, Thursday, something changed. It was as if all the fight went out of him. I'm sure deep down, he knew he was going to die. I was with him at the studios in Nottingham and he went round saying goodbye to everybody. He even tried to see his little Nottingham girlfriend to say goodbye to her. We came back to London and Gary had a few drinks in the pub but he wasn't at all drunk. Afterwards we went to visit some old friends of his and we sat up very late talking. We were too tired to drive home so they let us sleep on a mattress on the floor.

'The next morning when I woke up, Gary was gone. He was still there lying beside me, but I knew as soon as I looked at him that he was dead.'

At the inquest it was revealed that traces of alcohol and heroin had been found in Gary Holton's body, enough to have killed him. I found the heroin part strange, because Gary had been adamant about not taking drugs when I spoke to him.

Jahnette too finds it hard to believe.

'I can't understand it,' she said. 'Gary wasn't a saint but he hadn't had much to drink that night and he certainly didn't have another drink after leaving the pub. As for drugs, they said he must have taken the heroin an hour before he died. But I found him at about 9.00 in the morning. We were sleeping on a single mattress and my arm was still across his body. He couldn't have got up without me knowing. I think he died because he'd had enough. He lived very fast and he was worn out.'

Well it's a sad story. Gary Holton was a confused boy and the confusion surrounds him still. It's such a pity. He was so talented and when I was talking to him I realised that he was one of those rare people who have the gift of making people love him. Yet in the end it wasn't enough.

It's a great shame he was too busy to come to see me before he passed. Who knows, perhaps I could have given him some reassurance. But it was obviously not meant to be. I firmly believe that there's a time to be born and a time to die and it was clearly Gary Holton's time to die. At least he won't be lonely on the other side. There are so many other tragic young actors and pop musicians already there, he'll have plenty of company.

Chapter Three

'Come on Doris, up here.'

The rain was lashing down and it was a terrible night but I picked my way carefully up the rickety steps, now dripping with water, and onto the platform. They'd rigged up a canopy over our heads but the rain leaked through anyway and there were puddles on the chairs.

What a shame, I thought, they couldn't have picked worse weather.

Out on the sodden cobblestones the brass band was playing gamely and a damp Father Christmas wandered around trying to inject a bit of festive spirit into the proceedings. Considering the awful weather a surprising number of spectators had braved the elements and they stood about patiently under streaming umbrellas.

'I think we'd better get on with it don't you?' I asked the mayor.

So after a very few words I pulled the lever mounted on a box in front of me and bright fairy lights sprang out all over the centre of Halifax. Despite the weather it was a terrific thrill. I've always wanted to switch on the Christmas lights and in Halifax I had my big chance — although I must say I've got a suspicion that it wasn't me who actually activated the current. When I threw that switch there was a little pause, someone waved to someone else and then the lights came on! But why quibble, it was much more exciting than plugging in the Christmas tree lights at home.

I must say though that on such a night you couldn't exactly get carried away with the glamour of it all. Afterwards I noticed a mother standing there with her two children, one in a pushchair and the other standing next to her with water pouring all down his face.

'Hello Auntie Doris,' they chirped looking like a pair of swimmers emerged from the deep end.

Bless their hearts, I thought, and searched in my bag for some pound coins.

'Doris, can you do an interview now?'

It was a radio reporter, with all the equipment but nowhere to use it.

'Well I really don't want to stand out here in the rain, love,' I explained.

We looked around for somewhere dry and ended up doing the interview in the toilet!

Halifax was particularly memorable, not only because I switched on the lights but because I stepped straight into a controversy.

Christmas '85 was one of my busiest ever. My last book *Whispering Voices* was published at the beginning of December and suddenly I was plunged into a whirl of theatre appearances, interviews and events. Halifax was just one stop on my tour but while I was there I was honoured to be invited to switch on the lights.

It seemed a harmless enough invitation but it apparently infuriated the local Pentecostal church, which didn't think I should have anything to do with the lights, the theatre, or Halifax for that matter.

There were angry quotes in the local papers but I didn't fully realise what was going on because I don't have time to study papers when I'm travelling. It only began to dawn on me when I arrived at the theatre to find a great bustle going on. There were people queuing for tickets, people queuing to get in and people wandering amongst them handing out pamphlets.

We were actually making our way round to the stage door when I noticed one particular man who had a lady pushed against the railings and was waving a leaflet at her.

'Laurie, what on earth's that man doing?' I asked. 'Stop a minute, I want to talk to him.'

Laurie stopped the car and wound down the window.

'Will you excuse me, I want to go in,' we heard the woman protesting.

'You mustn't go in,' the man was telling her vehemently. 'You must not go in there. It's evil.'

'Excuse me, love,' I called sweetly. 'D'you think I could have one of those pamphlets?'

The man turned immediately. 'Certainly madam,' he said passing a leaflet through the window as if glad to find someone with a bit of sense. 'I hope you're not going to go in there.'

'It'll be hard cheese if I don't, love. My name is Doris Stokes and it's me they're waiting for.'

For a split second he looked stunned, then he recovered quickly.

'I've been waiting to have words with you,' he said eagerly. 'Do you know that you're the tool of the devil?'

He gave me the usual tirade that I've heard a hundred times before, but he wasn't allowed to finish. People standing close by heard what was going on and tried to push him away from the car.

'Don't listen to him Doris, we love you,' they cried and one woman turned on him furiously.

'Now you listen to me,' she shouted. 'The church has done nothing for me and I've come here as a last resort to see if I can get some comfort. So don't you start about the church. The church hasn't helped me.'

I didn't need to say a word in my own defence, the crowd did it for me. It was marvellous but Laurie was getting anxious.

'Come on, love, we must go or you won't be ready in time,' he said.

'There's 50,000 people around the world praying against you tonight,' yelled the leaflet man as a parting shot.

'If you were a Christian you'd been praying *for* me,' I said as the window rolled up and we moved off to the stage door.

'I can't understand it,' I said to Laurie and John, 'I don't interfere with their churches or decry their religion, so why do they interfere with me. And if they've got something so wonderful, why aren't the people queuing to get into their churches?'

Fortunately the disturbance didn't affect the demonstration and I was specially glad when one of the women who'd defended me so stoutly got a message from her little girl on the other side.

I don't want to give the impression that I cause chaos wherever I go but there had been noisy scenes a few days before when I visited Leeds. I was doing a book-signing in a big store in the city. It was a huge place on a corner and as we drew up I could hear the sound of chanting. The pavement was packed with people and they were holding a big black strip on which was written in luminous paint: 'I'm back by public demand!' They waved this home-made banner in the air and chanted 'Doris Stokes! Doris Stokes!'

It made me feel like a pop star.

We went into the shop, the doors opened and soon the queue stretched right round the block. How my arm ached after that session but it was nice to meet such lovely people. As we left they were back on the pavement waving their banner.

'See you in Manchester!' they shouted as the car pulled away. And sure enough they turned up in Manchester a few days later.

One of the nicest things about my trip to Manchester was meeting Julie Goodyear face to face for the first time. Julie Goodyear of course is the actress who plays Bet Lynch in *Coronation Street* and we've been friends for ages, but all our conversations have taken place on the telephone. Somehow, until last Christmas our schedules had never allowed us both to be in the same place at the same time, but at last we were able to manage it.

Laurie had booked John and I into Manchester's Picadilly Hotel and it was arranged that Julie would come over and join us for dinner on the Saturday night. Saturday night was about the only good night for going out because she didn't have to work the next day.

I was looking forward to it immensely but unfortunately by Saturday evening I wasn't feeling too well. I'd caught a slight chill from getting so wet in Halifax and my mastectomy scar had swollen up. I was sore and uncomfortable and couldn't stand anything tight across my chest. The thought of sitting for an hour or two in the restaurant in smart clothes was unbearable.

'Oh dear, Laurie, what am I going to do?' I moaned. 'I can't call the whole thing off now but I just can't face going down there like this.'

'Don't worry, love, it's not the end of the world. You can have dinner sent up here. Julie won't mind.'

So Laurie got on the phone to the restaurant and I went and changed into my best satin nightie and negligee. Loose nightclothes were the only garments that felt comfortable. I was glad I'd treated myself to a couple of glamorous sets. I mean you can't entertain the stars in an old plaid dressing gown and carpet slippers can you!

I was just combing my hair when the telephone rang. It was the receptionist from the front hall.

'Mrs Stokes? I've got a Miss Goodyear for you.'

'It's all right, I'll go and fetch her,' said Laurie, 'and I'll explain about dinner.'

Good old Laurie. John and I had a quick bustle round the room, tidying magazines and straightening cushions. We'd just about finished when the door opened and in walked Julie Goodyear.

I did a double take. I'd only ever seen her on television as the flamboyantly dressed Bet Lynch, and out of character I wouldn't have recognised her. Her long blonde hair, worn piled on her head on screen, hung loose round her shoulders and she was wearing a very demure dress in black and white floaty material with a big white collar instead of one of Bet's plunging necklines. She looked slim and elegant and anyone less like Bet Lynch would have been hard to imagine.

Then she opened her mouth and the old familiar voice came out, 'Eee love! It's grand to see yer!' and she put her arms round me and gave me a big hug. She did the same to John and the ice was broken. Underneath that cool chic exterior was the same old Julie I'd chuckled with many a time on the phone.

Laurie was right of course. Julie didn't mind a bit about cancelling our table in the restaurant and the dinner was a great success. Normally when you order meals from room service in a hotel, everything you order is brought on one tray and you're left to get on with it. But this time the management realised it was a special occasion. They laid on a waiter and waitress just for us and every course was served separately. It was like being in our own private restaurant.

The food was very good and it was a marvellous evening. We laughed and laughed. I haven't laughed so much in a long time and it did me the world of good.

Julie had arrived at 8.30 in the evening and we were enjoying ourselves so much she didn't leave until 3am. She's so witty she kept us in stitches and we can't wait until we get another free night so that we can do it all over again.

My appearance at Manchester's Free Trades Hall wasn't nearly so successful. The crowds were very kind and many people wrote to me afterwards to say how much they enjoyed the evening but as far as I was concerned I made a right mess of it. It brought home to me the fact that I'm not as young as I used to be and that it's pointless to attempt too much. Rest is vital to me.

The problem was that terrible wet night in Halifax. We were due to drive on to Manchester immediately after the switching on of the lights ceremony. This would give me the whole of the next day to rest before my demonstration in the evening.

Unfortunately we changed our plans. We were staying at a very comfortable hotel in Halifax. Holesworth

Hall is a lovely old country house set in its own grounds with olde worlde furnishings and an atmosphere of peace. Anyway after the lights ceremony I was damp, chilled to the bone and feeling very tired. The last thing I wanted to do was climb back in the car and drive for miles and miles through the torrential rain. I longed for my cosy room at Holesworth Hall.

'Quite honestly all I want to do now is crawl into bed,' I said to John and Laurie as we squelched back to the car.

'I'm glad you said that,' said Laurie sounding relieved, 'because I'm not sure of the route and I really don't feel like driving on a night like this. It's bad enough trying to see out of the windscreen without having to watch for road signs as well.'

Even John who is easy going and doesn't mind what we do as long as everyone's happy, admitted that he too felt like an early night.

That settled it. We abandoned the journey to Manchester and went back to Holesworth Hall.

Our unexpected return put the staff in a bit of a tizz.

'Oh no you couldn't possibly have your old rooms back,' they said. 'They haven't been serviced yet.'

We didn't mind we assured them, but the management did. New rooms had to be found for us to move into but it didn't take long and as we relaxed with a cup of tea by the fire listening to the rain pattering down outside we told each other we'd made the right decision.

The next day I wasn't so sure. By the time we'd packed up, travelled and unpacked again the other end, most of my rest day had gone. There wasn't even time for a nap before getting ready for the theatre.

Oh well, I told myself optimistically, I'll get through it somehow, and I suppose I did, after a fashion, but the whole thing was a nightmare.

I started off well enough, but then half way through I lost control. Names were pouring in from different directions so fast that I couldn't make out which part of the hall they were intended for. I struggled very hard to make sense of it but the audience, in their eagerness to help, made things worse. Usually I hear a name, then I have a moment or two to concentrate on that voice and I get one or two other details to go with it. That night in Manchester I was slow on the pick up and the audience unusually fast.

'I've got a Margaret here,' I said and just as I was asking Margaret who she wanted to speak to, half a dozen members of the audience started shouting and waving.

'Here Doris, here! That's my mum.'

'No here Doris! It's my Auntie Margaret.'

'No it's my *sister* Margaret.'

And so on until my head was spinning. Margaret herself was drowned out in the din before she'd had a chance to explain which Margaret she was and other spirit voices poured into the vacuum.

Finally in desperation I called on Ramanov to come to my rescue and together we managed to sort it out. The correct recipients were found in the end but it was a worrying experience.

I apologised to the audience and vowed that never again would I take on two consecutive engagements, unless it was absolutely vital. My power is just like a car battery. If a car battery runs down the car won't work and so it is with me. I must have time to recharge my battery.

December continued busier than ever but it wasn't all work. On December 20th the Spirit of Love Bus was finally ready for the official presentation and Laurie,

John and I went along for the ceremony in Tavistock Square, London.

We drove through the archway into the courtyard where the proceedings were to take place and there in all its glory stood the bus. It was lovely. Pale blue and beautifully painted, the words 'The Spirit of Love' stood out like a beacon along the side. On a dull winter's day it was a ray of sunshine and I was filled with pride at my achievement.

The special lift was down and a group of people were clustered round admiring it. The big-wigs from the PHAB organisation were there, along with the kids in their wheelchairs and Baroness Trumpington who was going to receive the bus on behalf of PHAB.

It was wonderful for me to see at long last the end result of all that hard work, but I think it was the kids who had the most fun that day. They wheeled their wheelchairs onto the lifts and rode up and down and back again. Within minutes they knew how to operate it better than the driver did.

Baroness Trumpington was very kind and gracious and she told me how marvellous she thought it was that someone as old as me should be involved in this way. I wasn't quite sure how to take that but I know she meant it kindly so I decided to be flattered.

After the presentation we went upstairs where they'd laid on a buffet of smoked salmon and wine. John and I exchanged glances because we don't really go in for fancy food, but one of the PHAB people noticed it and laughed.

'Now come on Doris,' he said, 'we know you only have a cup of tea normally but do try. It's a special occasion.'

So we did our best and it was very nice. The only thing I regretted was that I couldn't mingle with all the people. Since my stroke last year I've found I can't stand on my feet for very long and at these sort of do's I have to sit at the side and watch it going on instead of walking round and talking to everybody.

At around the same time as the PHAB presentation came one of the nicest events of my year, The Woman's Own Children of Courage Awards at Westminster Abbey. Apparently they've been holding these awards since 1975 when Mrs Mary Wilson presented the ten children judged to be the most courageous kids of the year with a special trophy. Over the years it's become more and more of a star studded occasion. At first the presentations were made by people with a political association like Mary Wilson, Audrey Callaghan and Margaret Thatcher. Then gradually a royal flavour crept in. Princess Alexandra, Princess Michael of Kent, Princess Anne and The Queen Mother made the presentations backed up by as many celebrities as could make it on the day.

But no matter how famous the names, nothing can steal the limelight from those ten brave little kids. They are the true stars of the occasion.

Call me soppy if you like but there's something about that day — the abbey all decorated for Christmas, the sweet sound of the carols and those special children all dressed up in their best, their eyes shining with excitement — that never fails to bring a lump to my throat and I wouldn't miss it for the world.

This particular year the ceremony was even more thrilling than usual because Princess Diana was presenting the awards. I have to admit that I'm an unashamed royalist and like a lot of other people there I was dying to see Princess Diana close up. All the celebrities were milling around. There was Ernie Wise and Peter Bowles, Shakin' Stevens and his wife who was expecting a baby in January. There was Su Pollard in all the colours of the rainbow, Claire Rayner and Lenny Henry, Rod Hull and the uncontrollable Emu (a great favourite with the kids), Dennis Waterman and Rula Lenska — oh and so many famous people it was very difficult not to stare.

Yet no matter how well known and famous the guests, everything stopped for the Princess of Wales. She outshone the lot of them.

When she walked in there was a sort of gasp. She looked absolutely breathtaking, and goodness me how slim that child is! She was wearing a violet suit with a fitted jacket, padded shoulders and puffed sleeves and a neat little pillbox hat to match. The deep colour emphasised the blue of her eyes and the fairness of her hair and she looked truly beautiful.

What's more she really is as marvellous with children as the papers say she is. You only had to watch her with those little ones for five minutes to see that it was true.

Quite spontaneously she picked up the smallest of the children, four-year-old Jamie Gavin, a tiny little mite and the youngest person to have undergone a heart and lung transplant, and she held him in her arms as naturally as if he'd been one of her own sons.

The atmosphere was terrific and those kids, well they were an example to us all. There was Sulas Kulkarni, a boy who'd gone blind at the age of seven, yet he played football, swam and went on a 700-mile bike ride to raise money for his school. There was Jodie Woodward who was shot in the face by a mad gunman and subsequently lost an eye. There was Sharon Allen, a leukaemia sufferer, and Sean Hedger who was only eight yet had saved his friend's life when the boy had fallen onto a live railway track. Then there was Joanne

Baron who saved an old man from that terrible fire at Bradford Football Club when the spectators stand went up in flames in minutes, Julie Malton who saved a friend from injury during a terrorist attack in Greece, Darren Durn who defied a gunman and ran for the police when the robber held up his mother's baker's shop and poor little Samuel Heenan from Northern Ireland who lost his mother from a stroke and then saw his father murdered before his eyes outside their farmhouse.

The most moving moment came when Steven Clarke a tiny six-year-old with brittle bone disease, received his award from Princess Diana. He'd suffered over thirty fractures in his frail little legs and he hardly dared moved in case he should fall and break another bone, yet he was determined to walk to the Princess. There he sat in his wheelchair, smart in a miniature suit and bow tie, with callipers on his legs, waiting patiently. Then when it was his turn he pushed himself out of that chair and slowly and painfully, each callipered leg an effort to lift, he walked the few yards to Princess Diana. It was the greatest distance he'd ever covered in his life.

'Well done Steven, well done,' said Princess Diana, her voice full of emotion and I found that tears were pouring down my face. I looked across at editor Iris Burton's aunt who was sitting next to me and she was crying too. It was one of the bravest things I've ever seen.

Afterwards talking to Ernie Wise I said, 'It makes you ashamed the way we moan and carry on about the least little cold, doesn't it? Here are these kids cheerfully accepting pain and operations and goodness knows what terrible things. They can teach us a lesson any day.'

I went home reminded once more that we should be

thankful for every day that comes along and so what if we've got a cold or a bad back? We don't have to make everyone else miserable too. It's a difficult lesson to learn and I'm as guilty as the next person about forgetting it. I seem to suffer from all sorts of aches and pains these days, I catch every bug that's going and I'm ashamed to say that there are times when I'm low when I moan about it. I whine on to John or Laurie or anyone who'll listen as if no-one else has ever had flu before. Then something like the Children of Courage Awards comes along or I meet some brave soul in the terminal stages of cancer and I'm brought up sharp. I'm glad Ramanov sends me so many reminders because I certainly need them!

I was very glad to get back home after dashing about the country for weeks, but it was only days to go until Christmas and once again I just didn't feel up to the preparation. I was exhausted. True luxury for me would have been to go to bed until New Year.

Fortunately Patrick, my dear friend who is also a chef, volunteered to cook the Christmas dinner for me on Christmas Eve, just as he'd done last year. It was such a relief. Patrick did the lot and he's such a good cook I didn't have to worry about how it would turn out. I knew it would be delicious.

And what's more, the spirit world had arranged a nice little Christmas present for Pat too. Patrick, who's Irish, lost his mother a few years ago and the previous year when we were setting the table I'd suddenly seen her face in a candle flame. Patrick's hair is darkest brown but his mother had a head of rich red chestnut and as her face swam through the flame, she said, 'Tell Patrick the candles are burning cleanly.'

The candles *were* burning cleanly but the message had a special significance for Pat. Apparently his mother who was a devout and superstitious woman always remarked when the candles were burning well: 'The candles are burning cleanly tonight, the souls are happy in heaven.'

This year as Pat was bustling about the kitchen he was obviously thinking back to 1984 and he went very quiet. I didn't want to intrude on his memories so I silently carried on with the mail. The mail doesn't stop just because it's the festive season. But after a while I sensed there was something else on his mind.

'Doris,' said Pat, coming out of the kitchen at last, 'I know you're very tired and I don't want to get you working but I've been so sad I've been dying to ask you this all day. Where's Mum going to be for Christmas?'

He was right. I was tired and I didn't really feel like doing a sitting but he had been so good to me I couldn't refuse.

I started to tune in when all of a sudden the door to the cupboard under the stairs, which Pat happened to be facing at the time, flew open, even though the catch had been left across, and a shaft of light flashed across the room in the direction of the bathroom.

Pat turned white. 'Doris, what on earth was that?' he asked fearfully.

'That was your answer,' I told him. 'There's no need to be afraid. Your mum's here with you.'

'What's the matter with you now child?' said a soft Irish voice distinctly. 'What's the matter with you now? I'm here when you need me.'

And then her voice drifted away. It was only a tiny episode but it cheered Pat immensely and he rushed off to phone his sister and tell her the news. So there were several happy Christmases going on around the Stokes household that year.

Chapter Four

John was very upset. He wandered round the house turning out drawers and cupboards, opening bags and envelopes and pulling books off the shelves.

'Whatever's the matter, John?' I asked when I came down from the bedroom and saw what he was doing. 'What have you lost?'

'My healing ring,' said John anxiously. 'It's vanished. I'm sure I didn't take it off anywhere but it's gone.'

John's healing ring, a lovely silver affair set with a turquoise, never leaves his finger and his hand looked quite bare without it.

'Are you sure you didn't take it off in the bathroom?' I asked.

'Positive,' said John.

But I checked the bathroom sink and the kitchen sink to make sure. Nothing. There was no sign of the ring at all. We searched the house from top to bottom, we looked round the garden and in the shed, because John had been doing a bit of gardening the day before, but we didn't find a thing. John was very upset about it. That ring was particularly precious to him.

He'd bought it some years before when we were in America, on the instructions of his Red Indian healing guide, Red Dawn. Now people are always asking why so many guides are Red Indians. Well they're not always Red Indians of course. Everyone has a spirit guide and they can be from any nationality at all. The one thing they have in common is that they are spiritually advanced and they have volunteered to look after a particular soul as he goes through his earthly life.

I don't pretend to have all the answers but I'm sure a lot of them are Red Indians because the Indians are such a spiritual people. They were probably the first spiritualists. Indians often used to go off on their own into the hills to talk to their spirits — perhaps they still do — so it's not surprising that with such a head start over the rest of us in understanding, so many of them should turn up as guides.

Anyway there we were one afternoon sitting in a traffic jam in New York when my eyes were suddenly drawn to a shop across the road. It was a modern place all black glass and red writing and somehow I couldn't stop staring at it. Strange, I thought, it's not the sort of shop that usually interests me, it didn't have any clothes or attractive furniture in the window, when suddenly Red Dawn's voice interrupted my daydreaming.

I hadn't heard Red Dawn's voice for years, yet I knew it instantly.

'I want John to buy something from that shop,' he said.

That was all, but we knew better than to ignore Red Dawn.

I glanced over at John and noticed that he too seemed transfixed by the same place.

'Red Dawn says you're to buy something from that shop,' I told him.

John didn't seem surprised. It was as if he sensed it too.

'Did he say what I'm to buy?'

'No that's all he said. But I expect you'll know it when you see it.'

The traffic was too bad to allow us to stop just then, so John went back the next day while I was doing some interviews. Apparently it was a Red Indian shop, filled with every touristy Indian item you could think of from full top-to-toe feather head-dresses to tiny silver and turquoise tie-pins. John was a bit taken aback by the sheer quantity of stuff on sale and he wandered round and round examining every single thing carefully because he didn't want to make the wrong choice.

At first, he told me later, he didn't know what to make of it. Then he tried the logical approach. Red Dawn obviously wanted him to have something that he would use regularly and that he could take home on the plane, John reasoned. That ruled out the huge feather head-dresses and the broad collars of brightly coloured beads. He wouldn't get much use out of them in London! It's got to be something small, John said to himself and he looked more closely at the tie-pins but somehow they didn't feel right.

He went round the shop so many times the assistant was getting suspicious and each time he ended up in front of a turquoise and silver ring in a glass case.

That must be it, John thought, and he asked to try it on. It fitted so well it could have been made for him and the minute the ring was on his finger he felt happy. He didn't want to take it off.

Convinced he'd found what Red Dawn wanted him to get, he bought the ring and he's been wearing it ever since, particularly during his healing sessions.

And now it was gone. I know John can be absent-minded at times but he'd never lost that ring before. We did our very best to find it but it was no use. Though we turned the whole place upside down we couldn't find so much as a gleam of silver. I was even beginning to wonder if Boots could have swallowed it.

I don't normally bother the spirit world with trivial things unless there's a very good reason, but John was so distressed I asked if they could help.

'Just this once, could you tell us where John's ring is?' I asked.

The reply was immediate. 'It's by the wall in the garden.'

'John come on, it's in the garden,' I told him.

The only problem was that we've got two walls in the garden, one in the back garden and one in the front. We searched along the back wall first and apart from one of Boots' old toys, we found nothing. Then we examined the front wall and there under a bush against the bricks, lay John's ring. It must have slipped off his finger as he was weeding and he didn't notice it was gone until several hours later.

I must stress that I don't often use the spirit world in this way, but by coincidence I'd called on them for help just a month or so before this episode. For several weeks I'd been suffering from a pain at the base of my spine. We all have backache from time to time but instead of getting better with rest, this got worse and worse.

The doctor didn't know what to do with me and I began to fear cancer of the spine. Day by day I grew steadily more uncomfortable until in the end I was literally crying with pain. It felt like red hot pokers being forced up my backbone. What on earth am I going to do? I wailed to myself, I've got a demonstration on Wednesday and I can't do it like this. I can hardly sit down.

In the end desperate for some relief from the pain, I called on my dad.

'Dad, what on earth am I going to do? I can't go on like this,' I told him. 'What's wrong with me?'

For a moment I thought nothing would happen and then at last I was aware of my father's presence. His love flowed out to me and I heard that dear old voice.

'Don't worry Doll, it's not cancer,' he said. 'You know your coccyx goes into a tail? Well the tail's turned in and it's trapped a nerve.'

'What should I do about it, Dad?' I asked. I couldn't face another operation.

'It's easy,' said Dad, 'and not at all painful. Get yourself a rubber ring and use it whenever you sit down. All you've got to do is lift the weight off the base of your spine and give the nerve a chance to heal.'

I was delighted. John went out and got me a couple of rubber rings. I covered them with pillow cases and put them on my chair in the sitting room and the other on my seat in the car. I even took one to the theatre with me the following week and placed it on my armchair on the stage.

The doctor, bless him, didn't scoff. 'Well your Dad could be right,' he said non-committally, 'it's worth a try. But if it doesn't work I think we'll have to get you into hospital for some tests.'

No fear, I thought silently.

And as if to confirm I was on the right track, a few days later I was clearing out a cupboard and I came across my photograph of Harry Edwards. I hadn't seen the picture for about two years. I knew I hadn't thrown it away but along with a number of other things it had 'gone missing' rather mysteriously when we moved and I was beginning to give up hope of ever seeing it again.

In case you haven't heard of him, Harry Edwards was the greatest healer I've ever known in my lifetime. He had such faith in what he believed the spirit world wanted him to do that he gave up his job as an insurance man and bought a beautiful mansion in its own grounds to serve as a healing sanctuary. The house cost £8,000, a great deal of money in those days and Harry had only £18 in the bank. Nevertheless he was so convinced that this was what the spirit world wanted him to do that he went ahead.

Donations came in to help him and every time he got desperate, something happened to get him out of the jam. Harry was obviously doing the work God wanted him to do. He never charged a set fee, he simply asked people to give what they could afford.

Harry's healing became famous, people travelled from all over the country to be treated by him and I have particular reason to be grateful to him. Years ago John became ill with cancer of the stomach and the hospital sent him home to die. In desperation I appealed to Harry for help and Harry managed to bring about a cure.

It's not surprising he had a special place in our affections.

Throughout the years Harry sent out little printed postcard pictures of himself with his healing letters, but I was honoured to receive what he called a 'real' picture — a large glossy portrait. I put it in a nice frame and for years it stood on the shelf in my sitting room. Whenever I felt under the weather I looked into Harry's smiling face and asked him to help get me back on my feet. Even when Harry passed over I felt that he was still healing from the other side and the photograph suddenly turning up like that just when I needed a bit of help seemed more than coincidence. As if to confirm it, a few days later I opened a letter to discover that someone had sent me a copy of Harry Edwards' healing prayer.

Harry's picture went back into the sitting room, I put Dad's advice about the rubber ring into practice and soon my back was vastly improved. The doctor had been so concerned about it he'd been on the point of making an appointment for me at the hospital, but now I told him it wouldn't be necessary. With the spirit world's help my back problem was nearly cured.

These incidents may seem trivial in themselves, but they show how close the spirit world is at all times. You don't need flying chairs and dramatic events. The spirit world makes itself known in the smallest ways.

Earlier in the year Laurie asked me what I'd like for my birthday. It's always a difficult question because people are so kind, they give me flowers and little trinkets and bath goodies throughout the year to such an extent that come birthdays and Christmas I can't think of anything I need.

'Oh dear, Laurie,' I said, 'I don't know what to suggest.'

Then suddenly I remembered something. A few years ago I did a sitting for Yolande Finch, the ex-wife of the late Peter Finch, a sitting that was memorable because they actually started having a row through me! Despite this Yolande was very pleased and afterwards she'd had some perfume made up specially for me. Apparently she went to an exclusive shop called Floris where they make perfume, and ordered some.

'Think of apple blossom and fields of buttercups and daisies,' she told them, which I thought was rather lovely.

Anyway the perfume was gorgeous and just before she left to live in California, Yolande gave me some more.

Sadly that was several years ago and I'd long since run out.

'Hang on a minute I've thought of something,' I said. 'I'd love some more of that perfume Yolande gave me.'

So Laurie went to the shop in Jermyn Street, London but they couldn't find a trace of the order. They checked their files very carefully but there was nothing under Doris Stokes. There was a perfume recipe by Yolande Finch's name so Laurie ordered that. It must be the one, he thought.

I unwrapped the handsome blue box on my birthday and took a long deep sniff of the perfume. Beautiful ... it was so long since I'd smelled the original I couldn't tell if this was exactly the same but it was lovely anyway.

A few weeks later I woke up suddenly in the middle of the night feeling very hot and restless and found myself facing the mirror doors of the fitted wardrobes. It was still very dark but the light from the street lamps slipped through the curtains and glowed on the surface of the glass. How those doors reflect the light I thought sleepily. Then my eyes opened a little wider.

I could see a face in the mirror and it wasn't my own.

'Oh dear who's that?' I asked.

Very deliberately I closed my eyes, counted to ten and then looked again. The face was still there but more clearly defined now. It was Peter Finch.

'Peter!' I said, startled, 'What do *you* want?'

'You haven't got the right perfume you know, darling,' he said in a distant voice.

'But Laurie went to the shop specially.'

'It's the *wrong* perfume,' he insisted and even as he spoke the face faded from the mirror and he was gone.

At that time of night I couldn't care less anyway, so I rolled over and went back to sleep, but when I woke the next morning I tuned in to check. I don't know if it was Peter Finch, or my father who answered my query but once again I caught the words, faintly like an echo ... 'the wrong perfume ...'

It was only a trivial matter of course but by now I was thoroughly intrigued so I rang the shop myself to see if I could get to the bottom of it. Manager Dominic Browne more or less confirmed what Peter Finch had told me.

'No, I'm afraid we couldn't find anything at all for Doris Stokes,' he said and he thought it was very likely that I'd got the perfume Yolande bought for herself.

'But Mrs Stokes,' he went on, 'I'm a great admirer of yours and we would like to make up some perfume specially for you with our compliments and from now on it will be on file so that you can order it whenever you like.'

I was thrilled. It makes you feel really special to have your very own perfume, particularly when you can order all the bits to go with it: the talcum powder and soap, the toilet water and bath oils, all matching.

I discovered that the shop is pretty special too. Apparently it was established in 1730 and it has preserved its genuine old world look. Inside it's all thick red carpet and glossy mahogany. The show cases came from the Great Exhibition at Crystal Palace in the 19th century and the lamp fittings are all solid Victorian brass. Not many shops in London can boast that sort of history.

What's more there's a 'by appointment' sign over

the door, so who knows — perhaps Prince Charles buys perfume for the Princess of Wales at Floris, or maybe the Queen Mother pops in for her talcum powder! It makes me feel pretty grand to think we might buy our toiletries from the same shop. Whatever would my old mum have said to think of her little Doll Sutton who thought a box of bath cubes from Woolworths was the last word in luxury, going shopping in the Royal Family's shop, just up the road from Buckingham Palace?

It brings it home to me just how far I've come from Grantham, that's for sure.

But as I said before, these things are of little importance in themselves except that they show how close to us the spirit world is at all times. I don't have to do a sitting or a big public demonstration in order to talk to spirit people. They are around us in our daily lives and half the time it's more difficult for me to shut them out for the sake of a little rest than it is to talk to them.

Yet no matter how hard I try to switch off, little bits still come creeping through. One day Patrick brought his friend Tony over to see me and unknown to me Tony was hoping I'd say something about his father. He didn't like to ask because he knew it was my day off but he was hoping just the same.

Of course his father on the other side picked up the signals that Tony was unconsciously sending out and came straight to my sitting room where we were chatting over a cup of coffee.

The first I knew of it was when I heard a persistent voice repeating the name Harry in my ear. I tried to close my mind to him but he was determined and I found my eyes swivelling continuously to Tony even when it was Patrick or Terry or John talking. What's more I was seized with an overpowering urge to sniff. I sniffed a couple of times but the impulse remained as strong as ever.

'What's the matter Doris, have you got a cold?' asked Tony.

I shook my head but I knew when I was beaten.

'Tony,' I said, 'does the name Harry mean anything to you?'

'Yes,' he said, 'that's my father's name.'

'And Pomp, Pom.' What on earth was Harry trying to tell me — it sounded like a pet's name of some sort. 'Pom . . . could that be Pomeroy?'

Tony was delighted. 'That's his second name.'

He was very pleased because it was such an unusual name I'd never had guessed it in a month of Sundays.

'I started him off in his job,' Harry told me proudly.

'Yes he did,' said Tony. 'He took me up for my interview.'

'And I bought him his first typewriter,' said Harry.

'Yes that's right,' said Tony, more and more amazed.

Harry went on to say how proud he was of his son because Tony is now an underwriter at Lloyds. It was only a few words, not a sitting at all really, but it meant a lot to Tony and by the time his father had finished speaking, he was in tears.

These things happen quite spontaneously and sometimes they seem so silly I feel a fool to mention them. He'll think I'm off my trolley if I say that, I think, but as often as not I get no peace until I do and then it turns out that the message was correct after all. Even that compulsive sniffing was wonderful evidence to Tony because his father had suffered from an habitual sniff.

I remember once when I was doing a demonstration in Brighton, Laurie and his wife, Iris, came down to stay for a couple of days. The first morning we decided to have breakfast together in our room and all the time I was getting ready, this tune kept running through my mind.

'I'm Henery the eighth I am, Henery the eighth I am I am. . . .' sang this irritating voice over and over as I soaped myself in the bath, and dressed.

Laurie and Iris arrived. The breakfast was brought up and still the tune went on. It got stronger and stronger until I could hardly concentrate on the conversation round the table. Every time I looked at Iris the volume seemed to increase until in the end I thought my head would burst.

'It's no good,' I said laying down my toast. 'Who the hell's Henry? It's been going on ever since I got out of bed this morning: "I'm Henery the eighth I am, Henery the eighth I am I am." It's driving me mad.'

'That's my dad,' said Iris almost dropping her cup in surprise. 'His name was Henry and we were always singing that song to him.'

That's all it was, just a tiny little scrap but Iris' Dad had obviously heard she was coming to breakfast and he wanted to let her know that he was close. His 'signature tune' was the best proof he could give her that he was really there.

We had a wonderful time in Brighton. The weather was reasonably warm considering the terrible summer we had last year and it always makes me feel better to be beside the sea. What's more I had a marvellous contact against all the odds during one of my demonstrations.

The evening had been going fairly well and lots of spirit people came back. There was a father who knew that his daughter always had £50 kept by for emergencies, apparently her mother had bought her a £50 ring on the understanding that if she was short of money she could always pawn it. There was a husband who knew that his wife kept his pyjamas under her pillow and touched them for comfort every night before she went to sleep, and there was a particularly tragic case of a poor man who'd walked in front of a train.

'Please forgive me,' he begged his wife, 'I can't really explain. I'd been worried and I'd had words with someone but I don't know what came over me to do a thing like that. After I'd done it I looked down at my body and thought, what have I done to my lovely wife and children?'

He'd left two children, he told me, and his wife, who was a nurse, confirmed this. Then he told me the gruesome details of his injuries, but they were so dreadful I couldn't bring myself to say them aloud.

'Oh dear I can't say that,' I told him. I turned to his wife. 'Look, love, you as a nurse know what happened, don't you?'

'Yes,' she replied, 'I know he was decapitated.'

So it was out. But at least I didn't have to say it and risk upsetting her if she didn't know.

The poor man just wanted to know that his wife forgave him and to make her understand that despite his terrible brainstorm, he loved his family.

There were lighter moments of course. There were grannies who wanted to wish grandchildren a happy birthday and one particular lady who said to her daughter:

'Give my love to Jim although he'll never believe I've been back when you tell him.'

And the recipient laughed because as she said, her husband Jim would never believe it.

Then towards the end of the second half a young

man's voice cut in very clearly, drowning all the other clamouring voices.

'I'm looking for my dad. He's called Norman,' he said.

It was so positive that I apologised to the man I was talking to at the microphone who'd been in the middle of a message from his wife, and called out:

'I've got a young man here who's looking for his father, Norman. Have we got a Norman here who's lost a son?'

There was a resounding silence. Then one man stood up.

'I'm Norman,' he said, but he hadn't lost a son. He was hoping for a message from his father.

'No, I'm sorry, love,' I told him. 'This is definitely a boy looking for his father Norman.'

Nothing. No one claimed him.

'I'm sorry, son, he can't be here,' I told the lad. 'Just wait at the side and we'll see what happens.'

The minutes passed and more voices displaced him. Then as always happens towards the end of the evening when I'm getting tired, the power began to fade and as it ebbed away the voices grew fuzzy. I strained to catch the faint words. It was getting more and more difficult and I glanced across at Tony Ortzen who was taking the chair.

'Not long now,' he mouthed.

Then suddenly the boy came back.

'My mother Barbara's here,' he insisted with unusual clarity at this stage of the proceedings. 'She's sitting over there. Please find her before it's too late.'

He directed my eyes to a bank of seats.

'Is there a Barbara sitting over there?' I asked.

There was a small pause, then a woman stood up. 'Yes I'm Barbara.'

'Come on down then, love,' I told her.

Tony was making signs that I'd have to bring the evening to a close, but somehow I knew it was important to speak to Barbara.

'Do you know Norman?' I asked her.

'Yes,' she said, 'he's my husband but he's gone outside for a smoke.'

'And have you lost a son?'

'Yes we have,' she said.

Thank goodness for that, I'd got the right family. It was difficult to hear what the boy was saying by now but I could just make out something about an accident. He was thrown, he said, and the back of his head and his neck got it.

'He went over very quickly, love,' I said gently. 'He went out and didn't come home again. He was killed.'

Barbara nodded.

'I feel as if he was thrown and the back of his head and neck got it.'

Barbara confirmed that this was true.

Then the boy went on to talk of someone called Anne.

'Anna,' Barbara corrected, 'his sister.'

There was so little power left by now that it was getting very hard for me to pick up anything at all, but the boy was still struggling to get through. He said something about his father.

'If only Dad could talk about it,' he said, 'if he could have a cry and let it out it would help. And if only they'd get my pictures out.'

I passed this on to Barbara. 'Don't shut him out of your life, love,' I said, 'he's still part of the family. Oh dear he's not been over very long, has he? Less than a year.'

'Only four months,' said Barbara.

70

Tony Ortzen was making quite urgent signs to me now to wind things up and the power was diminishing by the second but still the boy hung on.

'He hasn't mentioned his other sister,' said Barbara.

Faintly I heard the name Caroline.

'It's not Caroline is it?' I asked.

'Yes that's right!' said Barbara delighted.

Then there was a stir at the end of the aisle and I saw a compact, stocky man with a sheaf of papers under his arm striding purposefully towards the stage. Such was his air of determination I thought he was about to deliver a writ or something.

'There's Norman!' cried the boy in my ear. 'Come on Dad. I want to tell him I'm here.'

Norman reached us just as the power evaporated altogether. His son only managed to get one last message through to him.

'Dad wears my sweater in the garden.'

Norman was astonished.

'This is incredible,' he said. 'Yes I do wear his sweater in the garden.'

Barbara quickly relayed to him all the things their son had said and Norman looked quite dumbfounded.

'Well if all this is true, I'm staggered,' he muttered.

Afterwards they came forward to talk to me and Norman explained why he hadn't been in the room when the message came through. Apparently ever since their son had been killed in an accident they'd been trying to find proof that he lived on somewhere. Sadly they'd found no evidence at all. Reluctantly Norman had come to my demonstration as a last resort but by the second half he lost patience.

'This is a load of rubbish,' he said in disgust, 'I'm going out for a smoke.' He went outside and paced around the foyer smoking cigarette after cigarette and telling everyone he saw what a load of nonsense it was.

He was gone so long he didn't hear his son calling his name and by the time he got back into the hall the whole thing was nearly over.

Nevertheless Norman was delighted with the evidence that had come through, even though he heard most of it at second hand.

So interested did he become that the following Saturday when we arrived for my next demonstration, we found Norman and his whole family waiting at the stage door.

'You're an amazing lady, Doris,' said Norman. 'It was so good we've decided to come again.'

Sadly their son didn't manage to get through a second time but the family wasn't too disappointed. When we finally emerged from the theatre much later that night, there was Norman waiting to say goodbye.

'I just wanted to give you this, Doris,' he said and he pressed some money into my hand to buy flowers for my spirit children, together with a letter. This is what it said:

Dear Doris,

We were absolutely devastated by Joseph's accident and we decided that we had to consider the possibility that he was not gone forever. As a cynic this contradicts my logical approach to life, but I felt that now was the time to find out once and for all.

My disillusionment increased as I was told by various mediums and clairvoyants that I was enjoying a particularly pleasant and happy period!!

I finally determined to go to the top as a last attempt (your meeting) and then if I could get no confirmation that Joe was still with us, we would drop the quest for all time and seek to repair our shattered lives.

Knowing the great relationship that we had with Joe would, if possible, establish a basis for contact, we willed Joseph to be at your meeting because we were going to attend it as well.

The first half of that evening was hard work for you and as it progressed I began to fear that once again we had achieved nothing — so much so, that I left the hall for a smoke.

That's typical of Joe! He attempted to befuddle your performance and then waited until I had left before he really made known his presence.

We were seeking confirmation that life does not cease at death. You do not know us and had never met us until last Thursday. You had no association nor any information about us from any source whatsoever. You could have received nothing from us mentally — I was not even in the hall, yet you told us precisely, when Joe contacted, that:

1. He asked for Norman (that's me — his father).
2. After some time he asked for Barbara (his mother).
3. He named Anna (not Anne) his sister.
4. He named Caroline, his other sister.
5. His main injury was to his neck (broken) by going forward.
6. He went out and did not come back.
7. He asked us to replace photographs that we had put away.
8. He was fond of himself (yes, he believed he was God's gift to Sussex).
9. He now had lots to do — intended to travel 'And it will not cost you a penny'.

Throughout his life I had always begrudged him spending and never ever paid him cash for his work and efforts.

You conveyed nothing that was evasive — we carefully (unkindly) gave you no prompting.

We are now in no doubt that Joseph lives and we can resolve our sadness and despair knowing that in due course we shall walk along the road again with him beside us.

I thank you Doris for all of us — myself, Norman, his mother Barbara and sisters Anna and Caroline and of course Joseph.

I hope we shall see you again but being aware of your commitments it may have to wait until we all pass over.

Don't forget — the invitation stands — cup of tea, a smoke and a nice chat, *wherever*.

Our kindest thoughts for all time.

Norman Knight

Chapter Five

I finished my last book, *Whispering Voices*, from my hospital bed, propped up against the pillows or sitting in the armchair beside the window looking down at London rushing past below, and playing music on my tape recorder for inspiration. It was an odd ending to a book I suppose, and since then a lot of people have written expressing concern, so I'd just like to say I'm much better now thank you.

The problem was a slight stroke. It came on one evening as I was watching television.

Strange really because the book was practically finished, I had my presentation to Princess Anne to look forward to and everything was going well. But that day, when I should have been full of energy and celebrating the end of months of work, I felt distinctly peculiar. I was so tired I could have gone back to bed for a sleep almost from the moment I got up.

Don't be so lazy Doris, I told myself. You can't lie in bed all day. And I forced myself to get on with the chores.

By evening I was more tired than ever with a nagging headache, but an hour or two relaxing in front of the television would soon put me right, I thought. I reached out to glance through the *TV Times*.

'You know I think that film we wanted is on the other side,' I said to John. At least that's what I tried to say to John.

'You what, love?'

'That ffff ... ffff film wwwww w ... w.' I stopped. It felt as if I was trying to speak through a mouthful of glue.

'What's the matter, love, is something wrong?' John was trying not to look alarmed, but suddenly I was pretty alarmed myself. The whole of my right side had gone strangely heavy and I could hardly lift my right arm from the chair.

'I th-th-th-think yyy ... yy.' I was trying to tell him that he'd better call the doctor but I couldn't get the words out. It didn't matter, John was at the phone and dialling the number even as I stuttered.

Fortunately I have a marvellous doctor and he lives close by. He arrived at the house in minutes.

'Well Doris,' he said once he'd given me an examination and got me to bed, 'I think you've had a slight stroke. I want you in hospital right away.'

I was horrified. I was being presented to Princess Anne the next day, 'but ddd ... ddd.'

John interrupted, 'She doesn't want to miss Princess Anne,' he explained.

Some doctors might have been difficult but my doctor has always been marvellous and well understands the importance of morale boosters to general well-being. He agreed that since I could more or less stand upright and since the presentation was taking place in a hospital, the outing would probably do me more good than harm. Afterwards however I must go straight into hospital.

It was a deal!

The day was exhausting of course but as I described in my last book, I enjoyed it immensely and afterwards I went into hospital with no complaints. But if I thought I was going to have a rest in hospital, it just shows how wrong a medium can be.

First of all I had to go for brain scans. Terry had had a brain scan after his head injury and when I told him on the phone one day that I was to have one too, he frightened the life out of me.

'Oh it's dreadful,' he said, 'You feel as if your head is going to burst. It's terrible. You're clamped into this headrest and you have to keep absolutely still. You can't move a muscle. It's awful.'

He frightened me so much that I got myself into a state and I thought, I'm not going to have it done. They can't make me. I'll refuse. I knew I wasn't being sensible of course and as an ex-nurse I should have known better, but I suppose I wasn't well and I was feeling over emotional. Fortunately a kind male nurse named Tim came to my rescue. I told him of my fears and he was very sweet.

'I'm sure it's not that bad Doris,' he said, 'but I'll ask sister if I can come with you.'

Sister must have agreed because Tim came with me and held my hand throughout the whole operation. The rays were coming down but Tim never left my side. And I discovered the brain scan wasn't nearly as bad as Terry had led me to believe. I suppose he was so ill when he'd had his that it seemed dreadful to him, but in fact I've had far worse tests in hospitals than that.

The brain scan was only the beginning, of course. My leg dragged and my right arm was pretty useless and I was put on physiotherapy twice a day, including

77

Saturday and Sunday, to get my muscles working again. They worked me very hard but I didn't mind. I was determined to overcome this stroke.

When I got back to my room after physio I sang along to the radio to help my speech and I sat for hours, flexing my fingers and then making a fist with my right hand and twirling my right foot and lifting my leg.

'You won't catch me walking with a stick,' I said as my joints ached, and I ran through all the exercises again.

It was frustrating at times of course. I wouldn't let anyone cut up my food for me as if I was a baby, so I struggled for ages with pieces of meat and as often as not the meal was stone cold by the time I got it to my mouth.

My speech was still infuriatingly slow and well-meaning visitors kept trying to help me out by finishing sentences for me — often with the wrong words.

'No no,' I'd splutter, 'that's nnnnnn not w . . . w. . what I m-m-meant . . .' and I'd have to start all over again.

Nevertheless I was improving every day and the flowers and cards that arrived constantly cheered me up no end.

One Sunday morning I went down to physio at 10.00 for my first hour of exercises. Thirty minutes into the session I was laid out on the table kicking my legs, when suddenly a porter came in.

'You have a visitor, Mrs Stokes,' he said.

There was something about the look in his eye, a kind of suppressed excitement, that made me say, 'Is it Freddie Starr?'

'Yes,' he said, a bit miffed that I'd spoiled his surprise.

'Oh well could you ask them to give him a cup of coffee because I haven't finished yet.'

'Don't worry, Doris,' laughed the physiotherapist, 'I'll let you off just this once,' and she helped me down from the table.

'I'll take her back,' said the porter.

'No, *I'll* take her back,' said the physiotherapist and I had to hide a smile because they both wanted to meet Freddie Starr.

In the end they both come up in the lift with me and as we approached my room I found we were trailing a line of nurses as well. The whole pack of us squeezed into the room and there was Freddie looking as freshly scrubbed and bright-eyed as a choirboy.

'I've asked them for some toast and coffee,' said Freddie after giving me a big hug, 'because I came out without any breakfast. Not for anyone else would I get up at this time on a Sunday morning when I'm not working.'

Freddie and I have been friends ever since I did a sitting for him and gave him messages from his old mates Alan Lake and Diana Dors. I've seen the loving, serious side of Freddie but I also know his sense of humour so I wasn't at all surprised when he suddenly walked around the bed, turned back the covers, undid his belt and started to drop his trousers.

The nurses stared at him in amazement, which is just what Freddie wanted.

'What are you looking at?' he asked innocently. 'I'm going to take Doris to bed and give her a cuddle and I'll do more good in five minutes than you can do in ten days!'

He was only joking of course but he was right in one way. That visit from Freddie was a real tonic and probably did me more good than a whole bucket of medicine.

Soon I felt so improved I was pestering the doctor to let me go home. It was particularly important because I'd promised Jimmy Young that I'd appear on his new TV current affairs show and I was determined not to let him down.

Reluctantly the doctors agreed that I could leave on Thursday. This was cutting it a bit fine because the show was being recorded on the Friday, but I knew I could make it.

Anxiously the producer phoned me.

'Don't worry,' I told him from my hospital bed, 'I'll be there.'

Shortly afterwards Jimmy Young himself phoned.

'Jimmy, I promise you I'll be there in the studio tomorrow night,' I assured him.

'But Doris you're still in hospital.'

'I know but I'm going home tonight and I promise you I'll be there.'

'Well we'll have a nurse waiting for you and a room for you to rest in,' said Jimmy because he's a thoughtful man.

'That's marvellous,' I said, 'see you tomorrow.'

Yet even as he put the phone down, I'll swear he wasn't convinced.

The next day, as promised, I got myself on the train for Leeds. To be honest I was feeling a bit grey and fluttery and very tired, but I'd recovered pretty well. My speech was almost back to normal, my arm was pretty good and the worst problem with my leg was that it had spells of shaking uncontrollably. It still does I'm sorry to say but I've had to learn to live with it. I simply warn people that it's not a sign I'm about to go into a trance or do something spooky and then I tuck it under my chair as far out of sight as possible. It's a nuisance but I know I can count myself lucky. Some people are paralysed after a stroke. At least I can get about almost as well as before.

Anyway when I got to Leeds I was whisked to the Queens Hotel where the programme was being recorded and sure enough there was a nurse and a comfortable room waiting for me.

Jimmy and the producer were very good. They needed to talk about the show but instead of asking me down to the studio they came to my room to avoid putting any strain on me.

'We won't take you onto the set until the moment we need you,' they promised. 'The air conditioning's broken down and it's like an oven out there.'

There was just time for a rest, then I diddled myself up as best I could and went downstairs. I was looking dreadfully pale and drawn but it couldn't be helped. At least I kept my promise to Jimmy.

It was an interesting show. Jimmy wanted to discuss the question, 'Is there life after death?' I was there of course to argue that there was, Claire Rayner was there to disagree and there was a studio audience with a wide range of differing views.

Claire doesn't believe in what I do at all but she's always very sweet to me. She kept saying:

'Doris bless her this ...' and 'Doris bless her that ...' but we had some heated discussions all the same and despite the fact that she's opposed to me, she is always very fair.

At the end of the debate she said, 'It doesn't matter if we stayed here till midnight, there'll always be some that believe and some that don't,' and of course she was absolutely right.

What I like about Claire is that though she doesn't agree with me, she respects my point of view and she's never abusive. When we meet she's always polite and friendly and just as she respects my opinions, so I respect hers. I can't understand why so many people fall out over differing beliefs, there is really no need for it at all.

Isn't it funny how, when you come out of hospital, you discover that you're not quite as well as you thought you were when you were in there demanding to be allowed out?

I'd been fighting like mad to go home because I felt so much better but that appearance on the *Jimmy Young Show* made me realise that I wasn't as strong as I'd thought. The discussion lasted only half an hour but by the end of it I was shattered.

'Right,' said my doctor the next day, 'no more work. You're to have a complete rest.'

And so I spent the next few weeks pottering about at home and concentrating on my exercises. The physiotherapist had been very strict about that.

'You must maintain your progress,' she'd said. So I bought an exercise bike and every morning to this day I cycle a few miles to get my bad leg working.

But I can't stand being idle for long. The letters were piling up and we had so many requests for demonstrations that as soon as I was well enough, Laurie booked one or two theatre dates, widely spaced so that I'd get a good rest in between. And around this time I met an old lady who really put me to shame.

One morning I opened a letter from a woman in Sussex. Her aunt was coming up to her hundredth birthday, she explained, and her dearest wish was to meet me. Was there any chance that something could be arranged?

I was touched. Fancy an old lady like that wanting to meet me, I thought, so I rang her up for a chat.

Maudie Smith was amazing. A little bit deaf but

sharp as a razor. No sitting nodding off in rocking chairs for her. She was still active, alert and full of fun. I did the tiniest of sittings over the phone and got a few scraps from her husband Charlie who sent his love, and also from her grandchild who'd been tragically killed. Maudie had been very disappointed about her husband Charlie. Apparently she'd intended him to live to be one hundred too, but he'd only made it to ninety-five, and she was obliged to get on with the centenary celebrations on her own. Nevertheless she forgave him his lack of willpower and was glad to know that even if he couldn't be there in body, he'd attend her party in spirit.

As it happened, the following week I had a demonstration at the London Palladium.

'Wouldn't it be lovely, Laurie, if we could get Maudie along,' I said. 'I'm sure she'd be thrilled to see the Palladium.'

So Laurie rustled up a couple of tickets from somewhere and we sent a chauffeur-driven car to collect Maudie from her home in Worcestershire. It was too far for an old lady to travel to London and back in one day so we put her and her son Chester up in a smart London hotel for the night.

Maudie was a walking wonder. Neatly turned out with her hair freshly done she was full of bounce and energy. The day before she'd been busy mowing her lawn she told me.

'Well it grows so fast in the summer doesn't it?' she remarked.

She would have been pretty good for seventy, let alone one hundred!

Unfortunately Maudie's Charlie didn't get a look in that night at the Palladium but it was an interesting evening for her nevertheless.

There was a man called Walter who'd had cancer of the bowel and he wouldn't go away. He kept popping up in the middle of everyone else's messages.

'I've come to see my baby,' he told me, wagging his finger in my face, 'and I'm not going till I've spoken to her.'

Fortunately his daughter came forward to claim him after a while and Walter was content to pass on a few messages and wish happy birthday to his two grandsons who were both celebrating birthdays within weeks of each other. This done he went on his way and allowed other people to have their say.

There were two other tragic young men who'd committed suicide, one of them by stepping in front of a train, and there was one lovely married couple — Jack and Margaret I think they were called — who came back together to talk to their daughter.

'They're giving me the name Janet,' I said.

'That's me,' said the girl.

A moment or two later came the surname Bennet.

'Yes I'm Janet Bennet,' she gasped, torn between smiles and tears.

'She was upset because she didn't say goodbye to me,' Janet's mother told me and as she came close I felt a pain in my chest.

'Did your mother have heart trouble?' I asked Janet.

'Yes she'd suffered from heart trouble for quite a while, then she had an accident and a cardiac arrest.'

'I would have been a cabbage if I'd lived,' said Margaret. 'It was so stupid. I didn't even get across the road.'

Then she said something I couldn't quite catch. I could only make out the word 'bank'.

'She's saying something about a bank, Janet,' I

explained. 'Do you live near a bank?'

'No, but she had the accident outside the bank.'

'And she says she only had about £200 to leave.'

'Yes that's right.'

Margaret went on to talk of Janet's husband Steven and her son Rob. She asked for some flowers for Janet because her wedding anniversary was coming up.

'Next month,' said Janet in delight.

And she knew about the car they'd recently bought. 'You know what, you don't have to wind the windows down, you just press a button and they go up and down by themselves.' Margaret was highly impressed.

By now Janet was giggling happily. 'Yes the new car's got electronic windows,' she confirmed.

And so it went on and on. After the intermission, Tony Ortzen called Maudie onto that famous stage where we presented her with a big bouquet of flowers and a framed photograph from the new book. The entire audience, hundreds and hundreds of them lining the plush red balconies, sang Happy Birthday. It was a wonderful moment and I believe Maudie had the time of her life.

Afterwards she wrote me a lovely letter. She had had a marvellous birthday, she explained, she'd heard from the Queen and Margaret Thatcher and the whole village had organised a special party for her, but the best part of all was coming to the Palladium. Apparently she hasn't stopped talking about it since.

As usual, during that Palladium demonstration, there were several names and messages that fell on stoney ground. No one claimed them from the audience and I, along with most people present, had to assume that I'd made a mistake. I am only human after all and I do get things wrong. But not long ago we heard from a woman who'd attended a Palladium demonstration shortly after Maudie's and she was able to throw some interesting light on the subject of unclaimed messages.

I'll let Mrs Howlett from Essex explain for herself what happened:

I lost my husband last year from cancer of the bowel and I went to the Palladium with my daughter Lorraine, more for her sake than anything. I thought it was a load of rubbish. I would have liked to believe it but I couldn't. Yet I was half hoping that Doris would convince me all the same.

Anyway we sat there through the first half and all these messages were coming through and it was amazing. But I couldn't believe it.

'It must be a set up,' I said during the interval. 'She must know these people. They must have arranged it beforehand.'

I was going on like that when the man behind me tapped me on the shoulder.

'What are you taking that seat up for it that's how you feel,' he said. 'If you don't believe her after what you've seen you'll never believe anything.'

'Look I'm sorry but I won't believe it till she says something to me,' I told him.

After the interval there was question time and then Doris started the messages again.

'I've got a man here who passed with cancer of the bowel and he's asking for Laurie,' she said, and as she spoke she was tapping the side of her chair and rubbing her stomach, just like George used to do towards the end when he was in pain.

At first Doris thought she wanted a boy called Laurie but then she said, 'No, it's a girl's name.'

George always called Lorraine 'Lorri' but neither of us moved.

'He's talking about Annie Winifred,' Doris went on. Annie Winifred was my sister-in-law who died a few years ago.

Then Doris mentioned Rosie or Rosine. Well George's sister is called Rose.

'And he's looking for someone whose name ends in 'een'. Doris said, 'I couldn't catch the beginning, it could have been Cathleen, Eileen, een, een. No, sorry, I missed it.'

My name's Gwendoline. She also mentioned baby Peter who'd been born after he passed. Our Peter was born six weeks after George died. And finally she said she was getting the number 14 very strongly. Well I live at number 14, my daughter lives at number 14 and my other daughter lives at 194 and if you add those numbers together it comes to 14.

'That's Dad,' said Lorraine and she was in tears. 'Come on Mum let's go down.'

But I couldn't move. I felt completely numb, so Lorraine went down by herself. Unfortunately by the time she got to the front, a big family who took up practically the whole of the first row had got a message and they spent so long at the microphone that when Lorraine eventually got there Doris had lost contact with my husband.

She was very disappointed but I must admit the messages we did get amazed me. I hardly said a word all the way home. There's no way Doris could have known all those things. She'd never seen or heard from me. I'd never even written her a letter. I only went to please my daughter.

Now I wish I'd got up when she first mentioned

my husband but I was too shocked to move.

I think Gwendoline's story must be the tip of the iceberg as far as unclaimed messages go. Of course I do get things wrong now and then, it would be dishonest to pretend I didn't, but just as often, I believe, I'm right and people are too shy or stunned to come forward. It's such a pity when you think of all the effort their spirit people have made to contact them — in vain. And it seems that Gwen's husband has been trying to let her know that he's all right almost from the day he went over:

'Yes some strange things have happened,' said Gwen. 'They're only little things but important to me. The day George died, the vicar came round and asked what hymns we would like at the funeral. Now George liked to get up and sing when he'd had a few drinks at the pub and he always rounded off his songs with *You'll Never Walk Alone.* It was like his signature tune, so after I'd chosen a couple of hymns I asked for this song but the vicar advised against it. It wasn't a proper hymn, he said, and since there were going to be so many of George's friends there he felt it would be too emotional.

'Anyway the funeral was in the morning and afterwards I just left the house as it was and went to my daughter's but she couldn't face going straight home either.

'"I want to do something out of the ordinary, Mum," she said. She was expecting a baby at the time, so even though there was snow on the ground and we were still in our black clothes, we went to Southend to buy the baby's pram. And while we were choosing one, Elvis Presley came over the loud speakers singing *You'll Never Walk Alone.* So George got his song on the day of the funeral after all.

'Some time after this I was sitting in the conservatory that my husband finished building before he died, with a couple of friends. Suddenly as we were talking we all heard the front door open and someone walk in. As a joke, I said, "That's my George. Come in George." But my friend's husband was so worried that an intruder had got in he went upstairs to check. There was no one there.

'Just after this everyone started remarking on a strong smell of geraniums. I couldn't smell anything myself because I had a heavy cold but during the evening a neighbour popped in and she too mentioned the smell of geraniums.

'There weren't any geraniums in the conservatory but while he was building it, George had climbed over the dividing wall between our two houses and trampled our neighbour's geraniums. She had given him a good telling off about it.

'Now I don't know if this makes sense to anyone else but it all seems like more than coincidence to me. What's more, George often worked away from home when he was alive and I used to be afraid on my own in the house. Yet funnily enough, since he died I've never been frightened. It's as if George is still with me.'

Well there's only one thing I can say to that — of course he is! Some people might dismiss all these things as coincidence but to me it's absolutely plain. Gwen's husband, clearly a warm, loving man, is still close to her and has been trying to set her mind at rest by showing her as best he can that he's there.

What a pity Gwen didn't get up at the Palladium — but at least George got a few words in anyway. Now she wants to come to another demonstration in the hope that George will get through again.

'And if he does,' said Gwen, 'you won't catch me staying in my seat this time.'

I do hope she's lucky.

These days I tend to use what energy I've got for big public demonstrations. I do still do a few private sittings when the spirit world tells me that a particular case is specially urgent, but now I'm getting on a bit I can't do as much as I used to and I've had to cut down a little. I can reach as many people in one evening at a theatre as I could reach in two or three months of private sittings, so this seems a more sensible way to use my powers.

I know I'm always running on about how the world would be a better place if everyone learned to love each other. As Ramanov keeps telling me, if each one of us lit up his own little corner, think what an effect it would have as that light spread around the world.

You see there I go again! But at the risk of being boring, it's true, and it's wonderful for me to know that my words haven't fallen on deaf ears.

At public demonstrations I'm always struck by the love and warmth that's generated and by the unselfish way people not lucky enough to receive messages themselves, nevertheless pour out sympathy and good will to those who have and whose tragic stories unfold at the microphone. I know there are millions of nice people in the world because I meet so many of them at my theatres.

Not long ago I appeared at Lewisham, one of my regular venues because it's not far from home. I was staggered to discover that in bitterly cold weather the people were queuing from four in the morning for tickets. It was so cold that the management set out a trolley with free tea, coffee and hot soup to keep people warm.

'Well we've learned from you Doris,' said the manager. 'It's the people who count.'

I was really touched, even more so when I received a couple of letters afterwards echoing his words.

'We were queuing for hours,' wrote a lady who'd stood for ages in that freezing wind, 'but there was no anger, no pushing or shoving. We all had a joke and made friends with each other and talked about you and your books and how marvellous the atmosphere was going to be.'

'Despite the weather we had a good laugh,' wrote someone else. '"If we have to stand here much longer we'll be talking to Doris from the other side," joked the woman standing behind me ...'

And another lady added: '... the lovely part was that when we got into the theatre on the night, we were all waving to each other across the auditorium and meeting up with friends we'd made in the queue.'

With such wonderful people in the audience I knew it would be a special night and to cap it all, Freddie Starr turned up during the afternoon as I was getting my hair done.

'Oh Freddie, I'm getting ready for the theatre,' I explained.

'Are you?' he said, his blue eyes clouding for a moment. Then he brightened. 'I know, if I can lie down on the bed for a couple of hours and have a rest, I'll go with you!'

So this big star went up to rest on Terry's bed while the hairdresser battled with my springy hair and then he accompanied us to the theatre, fussing over me like a mother hen. He helped me up and down the stairs, wrapped me in my shawl so that I didn't catch cold and brought me hot tea in the dressing-room. After all that there wasn't even a seat for him. Every single seat had been sold, so he had to sit on a plastic chair in the wings.

There was plenty of variety that night, that's for sure. We had a couple of dogs put in an appearance to prove that pets live on just the same as their human masters. We had a woman who wanted a good moan about her daughter-in-law:

'I never liked her. I always said she was no good,' she gossiped to me though I didn't dare repeat it. 'I'm glad she's not in the family any more. The divorce was a good thing I say.'

Then there was a chirpy voice which announced, 'They called me Whack, you know.'

Whack? What a peculiar name I thought.

'Well me name was Walter really but they called me Whack.'

'Does anyone here know a Walter called Whack?' I asked doubtfully.

There was no reaction for a moment or two, then Walter's niece emerged from the audience.

'He's talking about the Nags Head pub.'

'Yes that's where he used to drink in his younger days.'

'And he says did you find me bank books?'

His niece laughed. 'Yes we did. There were two of them down the side of the settee!'

The audience enjoyed Walter. He was a bit of fun, but earlier in the evening they'd been just as appreciative for a very special mum.

The spastic boy she'd cared for for 41 years came back to thank her for all her devotion.

'They wanted to put me in the hospital, and they wanted to put me in a home, but my mum wouldn't let them,' he said. 'She looked after me right up until the day I came over.'

He wanted her to know that he was with Richard who'd passed not long after him.

'And oh Mum, if you could see me now. The arms that were twisted are gone and everything is straight now. I always had a good brain but it was just my body that let me down and that's been put right now.'

'Could my mum have some flowers as a thank you for all those years?' he asked me.

'Yes of course she can, love,' I told him. 'She certainly deserves them.'

Then there was a husband who was worried about his wife. She was having trouble with her neighbours who kept a big fierce dog which barked all day long. She was terrified of the dog but whenever she complained about it the neighbours refused to take her seriously.

'I had a breakdown Doris and was given psychiatric treatment and now they're telling me I'm imagining it. Even the police won't listen.'

'She's not imagining it,' said her husband angrily. 'She's scared to death of that dog. Tell her to throw a bucket of water over it next time it barks. She'll only have to do it a few times and it'll learn.'

More seriously still, I picked up two boys who'd been murdered, both of them stabbed. One wanted to send his love to his fiancée.

'We were going to get married in April,' he told me angrily, 'and then this happened. I left her at 11.30 and not long afterwards I was stabbed in the back. All I had on me was £10.'

The other boy whose name was Pat was looking for his mother Linda. He too had been stabbed late at night.

'What did we do to deserve it?' they both asked pitifully.

And I couldn't answer. We live in a very sick world these days.

It was a sombre note to end on but the power was fading away and I couldn't do much to lighten the atmosphere. Fortunately this particular night I didn't have to, because Freddie Starr was waiting in the wings to do it for me.

'Now don't all rush off,' I told the audience, 'because we've got somebody very special to present the flowers tonight . . .'

Then Tony Ortzen, the chairman, tantalisingly introduced John and then gave Freddie Starr a long teasing build-up.

'A star in more ways than one,' he hinted, but then gave the game away. He mentioned the messages I'd given our mystery guest from Alan Lake and Diana Dors. That did it.

The people in the audience who'd read my book guessed immediately who he was referring to and the place erupted into great cheers and applause.

Freddie, beaming all over his face and clowning about, bounced into the lights. He was marvellous. He handed out the flowers with a kiss for every single recipient, he patiently posed for endless photographs and then right at the end as the recipients moved back to their seats, he sang Love me Tender Love Me Do, in his brilliant impression of Elvis Presley.

Freddie has a beautiful voice and as the moving words soared out over the audience you could have heard a pin drop.

It was a magical end to a magical evening.

But backstage the fun wasn't over yet. All through the evening I'd noticed Tony and Janet Roffey sitting in the front row. Readers of my last book will know that they are the parents of little Hollie Roffey, the youngest child to have a heart transplant.

I'd met them before poor little Hollie was born, I'd tried to comfort them at the funeral and then a few months afterwards I'd almost given away the secret of Janet's new pregnancy. She was saving it as a Christmas present for her husband.

Well Hollie turned up on the stage that night. She was a lot bigger than when I'd first seen her but she was just as gorgeous. She stood there holding onto my knee and smiling up at me, the lights streaming down onto her rich copper head, bright as a new chestnut.

Oh dear, shall I say anything? I wondered. It was so difficult. I didn't know the Roffeys were coming that night but if I spoke up people would remember my book and say it was fixed. So I kept quiet. It's such a shame that you have to take these things into account but there you are. That's what happens when you start getting on television and in the papers. People can't wait for an excuse to criticise.

So I kept silent about Hollie but afterwards I met Tony and Janet in the dressing-room and we had a good old chat.

Janet was looking wonderful. She'd had her hair cut and styled and happiness had turned her into a really beautiful girl. Just as I'd predicted months ago when both those poor kids were in the depths of grief, their second child wasn't long in coming and she was in perfect health.

Little Samantha was born in the summer of 1985. She was just as gorgeous as Hollie, but dark like her daddy while Hollie took after her uncle.

'We want to give you a picture to keep,' said Janet, 'but we didn't know which one to choose so we've brought the lot. Pick out the one you'd like and we'll get it framed.' She put the whole set of photographs into my lap. I sat there looking through snap after snap of the beautiful gurgling baby. They were all lovely, but finally I made my choice and now I'm looking forward to receiving the framed picture for my mantelpiece.

It's nice to have such a happy ending to a story that started with tragedy, and now I am delighted to learn that Hollie has been given the ultimate accolade, which Robert Maxwell, the publisher of my books, put in motion. A rose has been named after her, so she will never be forgotten.

I'm sure that from now on things will go well for Tony and Janet. They deserve it.

Chapter Six

It was a beautiful day in the middle of summer. Battersea Park echoed with the shrieks of children at play, and a young family on holiday from Essex strolled under the trees.

'Can we feed the birds now, Mum?' the small boys pestered, until at last their mother gave in and produced a packet of stale bread from her handbag.

Soon they were surrounded by fat London pigeons, almost too overweight to get off the ground and the bread was pecked up in minutes.

'Now don't throw that bag on the ground,' said the father sharply as the boys cast about for something else to do. 'There's a bin over there.'

So one of the boys picked up the bag and trotted obediently over to the litter bin.

And that was when their pleasant day in the sun turned to horror.

There was an interesting looking bundle amongst the rubbish in the bin. Wrapped in a thick plastic bag it showed odd lumps and bumps and knobbles. Quite what the shape reminded him of the boy couldn't say.

He poked the bundle experimentally.

There was a rustle of plastic, the bag parted slightly and the boy found himself looking at a small human foot sticking grotesquely into the air.

'Dad . . .' he quavered, 'Dad . . .!' and then he was off and running as fast as if there was a fierce dog at his heels, to the safety of his parents. . . .

The new born baby had not died of natural causes, the police discovered later. It had been murdered.

It was a frustrating case. Despite exhaustive enquiries they had drawn a blank.

'Would you mind if I called in a psychic?' asked Debbie Martyr, the reporter on the *Wandsworth and Putney Guardian* who was covering the case.

The police didn't raise any objections so Debbie contacted Nella Jones, a clairvoyant, and then she telephoned me.

Now I don't pretend to be a psychic detective and as often as not although the spirit world does give information about murder cases which turns out to be correct, it rarely leads to the arrest of the culprit. But, if knowing these limitations people still want my help, I do what I can especially if the case involves children.

The murder of babies in particular is something that makes my blood boil. When I think of the agony I went through when I lost my son and how much I would have given to hold another baby of my own in my arms, I find it very hard to forgive someone who could deliberately hurt such a defenceless little creature.

'Well, Debbie, I'll do my best,' I said, 'but I can't promise anything.'

We live well outside the area covered by Debbie's paper so I knew nothing of the case and Debbie was determined to give little away.

'All I can say is that a baby has been found dead,' she told me.

That was all right by me. I'd much rather people didn't give me any clues at all.

I tuned in. For a moment nothing happened but I could feel the power building up and I knew there would be something. Gradually the outlines of my sitting room began to soften and recede and mentally I was somewhere else. I got the impression of a dank, comfortless public toilet. There was a very young girl close by.

I couldn't see her but I could feel her and she was scared, very scared.

'I think the baby was born inside a toilet,' I said, 'and one of his parents could be coloured or swarthy skinned.'

I paused. A new and horrifying impression was forming in my mind and I didn't like it one bit. I sensed that tiny body swinging through the air and that little head cracking against a wall with a sickening muffled bump. Quickly I blotted it out.

'I'm sure it's a boy and that he was murdered,' I said quickly. 'I think he was hit against a wall and I see injuries to the back of his head.'

I gave Debbie a few more details which we can't print because it turned out to be information only known to the police, and then I was being taken to another location. The feeling that I was being shown the place where the mother lived, flooded through me.

Looking inward, I saw a big building, high and gaunt and ugly. It was a shabby block of flats. In the distance I could hear the rattle of trains so I knew it was near the railway line and there was an overwhelming impression that I was between Wandsworth and Battersea.

Then the block of flats melted into the background and I got a confused view of arches or an archway, I couldn't seem to get that picture into focus, but there wasn't time to dwell on it. I was on the move again. Past the flats I went, to the corner of the road on which stood a pub; something to do with a crown. Perhaps the word crown was part of its name or perhaps there was a crown in the sign, I couldn't tell. I was being led on round the corner.

Here the road opened out a little and I could see an open space or small park not far from the pub. Somewhere on that open space was a public toilet which was left unlocked at night.

'Perhaps that's where the baby was born,' I said, 'and I'm sure the birth was in the early hours of the morning.'

Debbie was scribbling away without making much comment. Then I heard a name, very strongly.

'I'm getting the name Gillian or Julie. Anne might be part of it and also the name Turner.'

Whether this girl was the mother or whether she was connected with the case in some way I didn't know.

When I'd finished, Debbie couldn't really tell me whether I'd been much help or not, but she thanked me most politely for my time. First she had to take my report to the police. Afterwards however she explained that they seemed impressed:

'I must admit that I went into this with a very open mind,' said Debbie, 'but I was amazed at some of the things both Doris and Nella came up with. Although they didn't have any contact with each other their accounts tallied in a surprising number of ways.

'I was fairly cagey about the case but they told me things that I knew to be correct and also things that I thought were wrong but which turned out to be correct when I checked with the police.

'Doris gave details which haven't been released yet, like the exact injuries to the baby and the contents of the plastic bag, because there wasn't just a baby in the bag. She also gave some names which can't be mentioned in case they should turn out to be the suspects.

'Funnily enough she was right too about the name Julie Anne Turner. It meant nothing to me, but later while I was talking to the police, one of them was doodling on a piece of paper and suddenly he said, "Bloody hell. That was the name of the girl who was murdered six weeks ago."

'The case had been solved almost immediately and it got practically no publicity but the investigations into the murder of Julie Anne Turner had been carried out from the same incident room that was now being used for the murdered baby case.

'"One or two things right could be put down to lucky guesswork," said one of the policemen, "but all this is uncanny. It gives me goosepimples."

'As far as I know, they haven't solved the murder yet, but it was a fascinating experience. It certainly opened my eyes.'

There is a lot of debate going on in spiritualist circles about whether a medium's powers should be used in this way but I believe that when it comes to murder, everyone should give what help they can. Some people assist the police by helping in the search for missing children, others phone in with the tiniest scraps of information which might prove useful. My own gifts might not in the end lead to an arrest but it would be wrong of me to refuse to try.

A medium's work is certainly varied! A few months after the murder case I was called in to assist with another small but important aspect of mediumship — earthbound spirits.

It sometimes happens that after death a spirit is so tied to an earthly location — usually because of some traumatic event that occurred there — that he refuses to cross to the spirit world. He hangs around, sometimes for hundreds of years, making a nuisance of himself, particularly to people with great but undeveloped psychic power. When this happens the place is said to be haunted and receptive people often see ghosts.

Anyway it was journalist Michael Hellicar who drew my attention to the case. In my last book I described how I gave a sitting to one of Michael's readers who was 'haunted' by the 'ghost' of his dead wife. It turned out the poor woman had committed suicide during a depressive illness and she simply wanted her husband to know what happened and to stop feeling guilty.

Apparently, some weeks after the book came out, the husband contacted Michael Hellicar again. He had made his peace with his wife and had suffered no further problems with her, but recently strange things had been happening in the house. There had been flashing lights, objects moving of their own volition and most worrying of all, weird signs burned into the bedroom door. The man had also caught glimpses from time to time of ghostly figures.

It sounded bizarre to me but you can never dismiss this sort of thing out of hand, so Michael and I went down to investigate.

Michael arrived promptly one Monday morning and before we left I dashed into the bathroom for a moment's quiet to tune in, on my own.

Instantly the wife arrived. 'You got my name wrong when you wrote about me,' she complained, and she reminded me of the correct version.

As it happened we'd changed the couple's names to Brian and Janet to protect their identities since it was a distressing case.

'I don't mind you telling people my name's Irene,' she said, 'there's no point in hiding it.'

So from now on I'll refer to the couple by their real names: Irene and Trevor.

Once again Irene was worried about her husband. She feared he was heading for a mental breakdown.

'Please help him, Doris,' she said, 'if he stays in that house I'm afraid he'll go the same way as me.'

'I'll do my best, love,' I promised. 'Let's go and see what's happening.'

It was a grey, gloomy morning and the streets looked drear and water-logged. All you needed was a bit of swirling mist and the ghost film atmosphere would have been complete.

But Trevor didn't live in a remote gothic mansion. His home was a modern airy townhouse built around a grassy square and even the most vivid imagination couldn't describe it as a lonely spot. Trevor's neighbours were many and close and it was the sort of place where children would play football in the summer and leave their bikes on the concrete paths, and where the ice-cream man would call regularly.

Not the sort of location to interest a film director of course but then what most people don't realise is that new houses can just as often be haunted as old.

Inside, the place was neat, freshly decorated and not in any way creepy. Yet Trevor was obviously deeply concerned and his new girlfriend Pam was worried.

He took Michael upstairs to show him the burn marks on the bedroom door while I stayed in the sitting room talking to Pam. She seemed a lovely girl, friendly and open, but suddenly I wondered if Irene could possibly be jealous.

'It's not you doing this is it Irene?' I asked silently.

'No, it's not,' she said indignantly, 'I like Pam. She doesn't mind Trevor talking about me and she doesn't shut me out. They could be happy together if Trevor would leave this house, but they won't be any good till he moves.'

The channels were well and truly open now and as Irene moved away, a little boy came to take her place.

'I'm Kevin,' he said and as he spoke I felt a great rush of love for Pam.

'That's my little boy,' cried Pam in amazement. Apparently she'd been married before and had lost her baby son through a cot death.

The power was gaining in strength now and as I sat in the armchair sipping a cup of coffee, I felt the room slip away and I was looking at four big posh houses, and somewhere close by there was a priory.

'I'm Sarah,' said an elderly female voice. 'I used to live here.'

And then came a name that sounded like Rosenblaum or Rosenberg.

'Is it you doing all this Sarah?' I asked.

'No not me,' she said, 'I just want them to be happy.'

The next second I was pulled back to the present. Trevor and Michael returned.

'I think that years ago there were four big houses on this site,' I told them, 'and there was a priory nearby.'

'There was a priory,' said Trevor, 'it used to be about 250 yards away.'

And as he spoke I could feel the psychic power coming off him in waves, but it was clouded and confused.

rry and Boots: two souls that need each other.

lphi and Boots. Personal security? Asleep on the job!

Handing the Spirit of Love Bus keys to Baroness Trumpington. PHAB members look on.

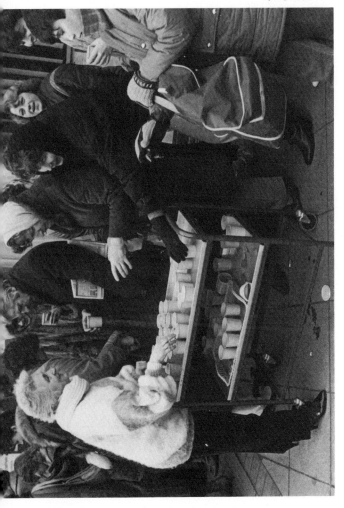

7 am: free soup, tea and coffee, courtesy of the Management to warm their bodies to match their hearts.

PHOTOGRAPH COURTESY OF STEVE HICKEY

Gary Holton: so much talent, left so much sorrow, now he's found a brighter future.

Julie Goodyear: the hug that says it all, a big star and my mate.

visham Theatre: Freddie Starr, John and myself – so much love, a perfect end
a perfect evening. PHOTOGRAPH COURTESY OF STEVE HICKEY

e London Palladium: Maudie Smith, a hundred years young. The audience
g 'Happy Birthday' as Maudie claimed it was 'The best day of my life'.
PHOTOGRAPH COURTESY OF STEVE HICKEY

'When he's away from home working, he suddenly stops what he's doing and has an overwhelming desire to get back to the house,' said Irene. 'It's as if he's on an invisible thread.'

Trevor confirmed that this was true, but before I could repeat Irene's warning that he should move, another spirit from the old days popped in. Dr Golden, he said his name was, and he too had lived in one of the big houses.

'The towel rail keeps falling off,' he told me, 'and the tap keeps turning on, but it's not me doing it. I couldn't do a thing like that.'

The case was becoming more and more puzzling. The house seemed to act as a magnet for every passing spirit and it could only be Trevor's psychic power that was attracting them.

'You must learn to channel your power properly,' I told Trevor and then my voice trailed off. The atmosphere was changing and suddenly I became aware of outbuildings round the back of the large houses and a feeling of anger and despair. My head was pulled to one side, imitating the position of the head of a hanged man and I realised that someone had hanged himself in one of those outhouses. I caught a tiny glimpse of a man holding his head on one side.

'Sam,' he said. So I took it that Sam was his name.

'That's it,' said Trevor. 'I keep seeing this man on the stairs. He wears an old dressing-gown and he holds his head on one side as if he'd been hanged.'

Sam brought with him such a tide of misery that I was reminded of Irene's words to me about Trevor:

'If he doesn't move I'm afraid he'll go the same way I did,' and I wondered whether she was telling me more than I'd first realised. Could she too have been affected by Sam's unseen presence and have been driven to commit suicide by unconsciously picking up his suicidal thoughts?

'Now listen to me, Sam,' I said firmly, 'you're upsetting these people. You've got to stop. If you look to the right you'll see a light. That's your guide. Just put your hand out and he will help you over. You're earthbound son.'

Black depression rolled over me, then I heard Sam speaking again in a dull, cracked voice, 'My child ... my child drowned.'

'Your child drowned?' I asked in surprise. 'But there's no river near here surely?'

'There used to be a pond on the old maps,' said Trevor.

'Well look Sam it's no good blaming yourself. If you go to the spirit world you'll find your little daughter ...'

'Madelaine,' said Sam.

'They called her Madelaine,' I explained to the others who couldn't hear Sam's side of the conversation. 'Go where the light is Sam and you will find your daughter grown up and waiting for you.'

There was silence.

'Are you going to do that for me, Sam?'

Nothing. He'd wandered away again. I only hoped he'd taken my advice and was following the light.

The silence grew and grew. There was no point in forcing contact, so while I was waiting I suggested that I have a look at the burned door.

Trevor's house was on three floors. The first and second floors felt pleasant and relaxed but as I climbed the stairs towards the third landing I began to feel distinctly queer. My body was chilled and my legs went all weak and shaky.

'This is where I see Sam,' said Trevor as we reached the top.

Then he opened the bedroom door and showed me the extraordinary marks. Defacing the whole of the centre of the door was a large, crudely drawn star of David scorched into the paintwork and beneath it was the rough outline of the letter 'S'.

It was the strangest thing I've ever seen. The burnt paintwork was quite smooth and silky to touch, apart from a tiny area near the top on which one or two small blisters showed, and the surrounding paintwork was unmarked.

I've seen some weird things in my time as a medium but nothing as weird as this. If it was Sam's work it beats me how he did it.

Shaking my head in bewilderment I followed Trevor back downstairs.

'What d'you think you're up to, Sam?' I asked silently, but there was no reply. Instead I got a picture again, but in more detail this time.

There was a large red brick house, a big gate at the bottom of the garden and two paths going out the back to the outhouses. There was a study with french windows and one of the paths skirted to the right of it and led round to a barn or a shed. This was where Sam hanged himself.

But Sam was silent. I could only hope that he'd taken my advice and was busy greeting his daughter in the spirit world.

'Well, Trevor, I hope he's gone,' I said at last, 'but there are two things you must do. You must develop your psychic power properly to stop them tapping into it like this, because you can't cope with it — and you must move. You're not happy in this house any longer and you won't be really happy again until you move.'

Oddly enough he seemed very reluctant to leave the place but he promised to think it over. There was nothing else I could do.

I hope Trevor's taken my advice and I hope that Sam has gone on his way. At the moment it's too early to be sure. We'll just have to wait and see.

Chapter Seven

Dear Editor,

I have been staying with my sister since November, missing my regular ordered copy of *Weekend*. I have just returned home and I'm catching up on my back copies. I was reading December 10th's copy and with dismay saw the article offering a free sitting with Doris Stokes.

I realise that my chance for that offer has long since gone but I would beg you to continue to read my letter and hopefully you may be able to help us.

My sister Gillian is 35 years of age, she is married with two children aged 9 years and 7 years. Gill has Chronic Myloid Leukaemia and has been in and out of remission since November 11th. Her consultant has now told her that she has only 9-12 months to live. Gill is a wonderfully brave girl and has terrific willpower. When she found out about her illness, indeed when we all found out, it shook our faith. We only regained that faith when we saw Doris on the television. Just watching that one programme allayed all Gill's fears on dying. She knew she would join Dad on the spirit side.

If Gill could have one wish before she died I know it would be to meet Doris Stokes. She still watches the video of that programme.

Dear Editor, I know you must know her home address. Would you please make a dying girl very happy and forward this letter to her. We would travel to the end of the earth for Gill, we love her so dearly.

Thank you so much for sparing the time to read this letter. If my request is impossible to perform please let me know so that I can keep trying myself to contact Doris.

Yours sincerely
Heather Randall
Staffordshire

At the moment I have a backlog of 20,000 letters, most of them asking for sittings and obviously it's not possible for me to do even a fraction of them. I worked it out the other day and I was amazed to discover that if I gave a sitting a day without a break for weekends or holidays, for the next 50 years, I'd be 116 years old and I still wouldn't have worked my way through them all!

Even with the spirit world's help and the best doctor in South London, I doubt if I'll make it to my 116th birthday let alone be working until then, so sadly we have to tell most of these people that a private sitting's just not possible. But I haven't given up sittings altogether. Now I let the spirit world tell me which of the desperate cases I must see. There's no mistaking the nudge I get from the other side. Suddenly, as I'm sifting through the mail, one letter will leap out at me, its envelope almost burning my hand and I'll know that Ramanov my guide wants me to tackle this particular case.

Heather's letter, printed above, was one of these.

Weekend magazine had approached me some weeks before to see if they could arrange a sitting for one of their readers. Knowing that so many people wanted to see me, they were going to ask their readers to write in saying why they thought they should be chosen.

I was a bit doubtful about the idea at first, but then I realised that some desperate soul would get a sitting and the magazine would handle the letters and make the heartrending choice. Believe me, at times it's agony to have to turn down one tragic case in favour of another. Even with the spirit world's help it's a nightmare task.

Anyway I agreed, a 'winner' was chosen, the date was fixed and then Heather's letter was passed on to me by the magazine. That day I had my usual stack of mail to sort through, but there was something about that deep blue envelope that caught my eye. It wasn't just the colour. No matter how I piled the letters that envelope kept falling into my hand and when I opened it and read Heather's moving words I knew why. Without doubt I must see her sister.

Laurie looks after my diary these days and makes all the appointments for me, so I phoned him at once.

'Laurie put them in,' I said, after I'd explained the situation, 'I don't care where or when, but I must see them.'

'It means working on your day off,' he warned.

'That doesn't matter,' I said. 'This is important.'

So one Thursday morning Heather and her sister Gillian made the long journey down from Staffordshire. Their train was late and they'd been travelling for hours but they didn't complain. Instead they were

111

full of apologies for having kept me waiting.

What marvellous sisters they were. There was Gillian, a lovely child, so brave but so pitifully thin even though she told me proudly she'd put on a stone in weight since going into remission; and there was Heather, compassionate and devoted. Heather was a nurse at the hospital where Gillian was being treated and on one occasion when Gillian was very ill, she'd begged Heather not to leave her.

'I won't,' said Heather taking her hand and she didn't. It's a wonder she didn't get fired because nurses can't stay at a patient's side as they please.

'I wouldn't have cared if I was fired,' said Heather. 'Gillian needed me more than anyone else at that time and that's all that mattered.'

How wonderful to have such love between sisters I thought, as I got them settled with a cup of coffee. So many girls fight and squabble.

It didn't take long to get tuned in. Sometimes I have to struggle for ages to build up the power and make a contact but Gillian's dad was so close to her, I found him immediately. He was so worried about his little girl, he rarely left her side either, and he was soon ticking me off.

'Put that cigarette out,' he ordered, minutes after we got started. 'It affects her lungs.'

Gillian hadn't liked to mention it but I stubbed out my menthol cigarette at once. Her father went on to talk about the family. He'd met Bill his father and Nelly his mother on the other side he said and he mentioned his wife Jan who recently had a gall bladder operation.

'She's worried because she still suffers pain. She thinks it's something serious but it's only adhesions,' he explained.

112

Then he said something about Gill having three children.

'No only two,' said Gillian.

'Three!' insisted her father firmly. 'Two kids and a dog. The third is the bloody dog. She calls him the baby.'

Gill burst out laughing. 'Yes I do!' she chuckled.

When she smiled her face lit up with such serenity and peace that I could see she had accepted the worst and learned to live with it.

Her father had not. He kept worrying that the illness was somehow his fault. Although he'd passed quickly with a heart attack he worried that Gill might have inherited some tendency through his genes.

'I want to know why,' he said. 'I've asked them over here and they say it's God's will and I say bugger God's will, I want to know why.'

He was also worried about his grandchildren, Christopher and Pippa.

'She hasn't told my grand-daughter,' he said. 'If the worst happens she must explain it to the children. Tell them Mummy had to come and live with Grandpa. But don't give up Gill. You've defied them up till now, because they said you wouldn't be here for Christmas and you bloody were.'

I tried to get him onto a more cheerful subject by asking what he used to do for a living.

'I used to do the buses,' he said.

'Do the buses?' I queried silently. 'D'you mean you were a bus driver?'

'No,' he said impatiently, 'I used to do the buses.'

Puzzled I repeated the odd phrase to Gill.

'Yes that's quite right,' she said, 'he cleaned buses.'

But her father didn't want to waste time on trivia. He gave me the name John.

113

'That's my husband,' said Gill.

'She's got one of the best,' said her father. 'He's breaking his heart but he tries not to show it. He goes and shuts himself in the bathroom and has a cry.'

I didn't want to upset Gill so I tried to persuade her dad to tell me a bit more about his grandchildren.

'Pippa's a beautiful child. Very graceful. She's always dancing,' he said, 'and as for Christopher, he's a good lad. He runs about after his mother doing things for her but inside he's scared. He could be clever if he applied himself.'

He went on to mention some more family names and the fact that he knew that Gill had recently been talking to someone who was discussing a divorce, but most of all he wanted her to know that if things went wrong and her treatment wasn't successful, he'd be there to take her by the hand and help her over into a new life on the other side.

'We're so proud of her, she's so brave,' he said before the power finally faded away.

Afterwards as the three of us sat chatting I tried to emphasise to Gill the importance of explaining to her children what was going on. I've seen grown men and women in their forties still scarred by the sudden loss of a parent, because they didn't understand what was happening.

'If Mummy suddenly disappears they can't understand it,' I said. 'They think she must have gone because they did something wrong and they carry that guilt for the rest of their lives.'

Gill promised she would do her best to explain.

'I have talked to Christopher,' she said, 'but somehow I haven't managed to say anything yet to Pippa. I will try.'

At the end, just as they were leaving, she put her

arms around me and gave me a big hug.

'I feel very bitter because I've got to leave my lovely husband and children,' she confessed, 'but Doris I'm not afraid to die after today. I know my father will be there.'

Tears burned my eyes as I returned the hug. She was obviously one of God's special children and had been chosen long before she was born to take this difficult path.

'Don't give up, love. Miracles do happen,' I assured her, and then they were walking away up the garden path, one frail, one sturdy, two devoted sisters.

I don't know where these marvellous people find their courage. There are so many of them. If you passed them in the street you wouldn't give them a second glance, yet their ordinary appearance hides a bravery that would do credit to the most heroic soldier.

I remember being very taken aback at a demonstration in Brighton when a spirit mother in the course of a message to her daughter said abruptly:

'She's going to join us shortly.'

That can't be right, I thought in horror. The young woman in front of me was only in her early thirties and apparently healthy and strong.

'I misheard you, love,' I said silently to the mother.

'No you didn't,' she replied tartly, 'she's coming over soon. She's got cancer. Tell her to put her affairs in order.'

That's all very well I thought, but how do I say that in front of hundreds of people? Not for the first time I found myself wracking my brains for a tactful way to phrase a difficult spirit message.

'There's going to be a parting soon, love, your mum tells me.' I said gently, 'Go and see a solicitor and get things put in order. D'you know what I mean?'

The girl nodded silently, too full of emotion to speak, but afterwards she wrote me a beautiful letter. She too was no longer afraid of death now she knew her mother was waiting for her, she said, and the message had given her the strength to consult her solicitor about all the little details that needed sorting out.

Strange really. Until a few weeks ago I'd always felt that one of my most important tasks was to help parents who'd lost children because I'd lost a baby myself and I could understand that terrible pain. I still believe this of course but more and more recently I've come to realise how much work needs to be done for the terminally ill. Perhaps it's just an illusion but to me it seems that their numbers are increasing and so many of them are desperate for comfort and reassurance.

Gill of course wasn't the winner of the *Weekend* 'competition'. The magazine made their choice and quite rightly didn't publish any details until well after the sitting. They were amazed at the response. Hundreds and hundreds of letters poured into the office and the editorial staff had the agonising task of sorting them out. They whittled them down to a short list of about twenty, then the editor made the final decision.

They kept the contents of the winner's letter secret of course, but afterwards in the report of the sitting, they included the extracts that so moved the editor.

'I would love so much to have a sitting with Doris Stokes to thank her for the comfort my teenage daughter gained from her books before she died in such distressing circumstances,' wrote Helen Bates. 'I believe they helped her not to be frightened when the end came. All her life Alison tried so hard to help and please people, even insisting on doing first aid duty at our local theatre while she was ill. It would be wonderful if Doris could put me in touch with her. I'd just like to tell her how much I miss her and how sorry I am that I didn't do more for her.'

Helen Bates, a comfortable, dark haired, middle-aged lady arrived with reporter Jack Pleasant and the magazine's photographer. All I knew about Helen at that stage was her name, but the moment she walked in the door I sensed great tragedy around her. She had lost a child I was sure of that, but there was something else. She was suffering not only from that awful searing pain, but from a feeling of guilt as well.

We started work almost as soon as the introductions were over. At once I saw a tiny light flickering around Helen. That meant the tragedy was recent.

'I can see a tiny light, that tells me someone hasn't been over very long,' I said slowly. 'It's not a year yet. It was a great tragedy and it's been harder on you love than on anyone.'

Helen swallowed hard and nodded.

Suddenly I heard a young girl's voice, she couldn't have been more than nineteen or twenty and she told me she'd gone over quickly at the end and hadn't said goodbye.

'That's right,' said Helen. 'She was only eighteen actually.'

As she spoke I saw a brief flash behind her head and illuminated in the light was a face that looked even younger than eighteen surrounded by pretty fair hair.

It turned out that the poor child had been suffering from a brain tumour and no one knew. Her behaviour changed and people nagged her for being moody, when all the time she was desperately ill.

'I didn't realise anything was wrong,' she said. 'First my eyes went funny and I got glasses. The doctor told me it was to do with my monthly cycle.'

117

'Yes,' said Helen her eyes filling with tears. 'She held her head on one side because she couldn't see.'

The young girl whose named turned out to be Alison, mentioned her grandad Bill, her dad Peter David and her boyfriend Jim. She even talked of a pet.

'It's called Cindy or Sandy something like that,' I said aloud struggling to catch the faint word.

'Cinders,' said Helen. 'It's a cat, born the day she died.'

Alison gave quite a few other names but she was chiefly concerned with easing her mother's feelings of guilt.

'If the bloody doctors couldn't tell me I had a tumour on the brain, how could my mum tell why I was so nasty,' she said. 'Remember me to Iris,' she added pointedly.

Helen gasped. 'That's a woman I work with. She was very cruel to her.'

'Tell her I forgive her,' said Alison. 'She's been worrying about it ever since. I hated her at the time but I don't now. She wasn't to know I was ill.'

But Alison wasn't the only spirit person to pop in during that sitting. Towards the end when Alison had grown tired from the effort of communicating, she moved off the vibration and a man dashed in while he had the chance.

'It's Jack James,' he said and the light whipped round to Jack Pleasant who had been calmly taking notes. Jack's jaw dropped.

'That's my father-in-law,' he said.

'I just wanted to get my two pennorth in,' Jack senior told me, obviously very pleased with himself.

'Oh and tell them I know what they're up to. They're having the builders in soon.'

'They're due next month,' said Jack weakly.

Afterwards he wrote a very nice article about the sitting, and included a verdict from Mrs Bates:

'Marvellous ... she even mentioned the big coloured photo of Alison I have in my bedroom and that her eyes seem to follow you around the room. It was an experience that will make these last few tragic months a lot easier to bear ...'

But I wasn't finished with *Weekend* yet. Not long after the sitting they contacted me again. All those heartrending letters had moved them as nothing had moved them for years. They hadn't realised how much grief there was in the world and they wanted to do something for all the hundreds of readers who hadn't had a sitting. Would I mind giving a public demonstration specially for the *Weekend* readers? they asked.

I was delighted to help of course. The editor suggested the 600 seater Mermaid theatre near the Thames in London but Laurie explained that it would be too small, knowing that I would like each invited guest to have a travelling companion. I felt this was especially necessary as I knew some people would be coming from Jersey, Cornwall, Scotland and even Italy. So we hired the 1200 seater Poplar Civic Theatre where I had been filmed for the 40 minutes TV documentary *A Happy Medium.* Once again the response was greater than expected for an afternoon demonstration, so I asked Laurie to hire an even larger theatre.

'We'll pay for it, love, it's only fair to the people. How can we disappoint them?'

So Laurie cancelled the Poplar theatre and booked the lovely Barbican Concert Hall in the Barbican Centre opened by Her Majesty the Queen in 1982. The capacity was over 2,000, yet the demand was so great we still had to disappoint some people. But we had to stop somewhere.

It promised to be a wonderful occasion and I was looking forward to being the first medium to appear at the Barbican when something happened.

A few days before the *Weekend* demonstration a reporter came to see me. I won't mention his name because it must be humiliating for a trained journalist to have to make his living by muck-raking so I won't embarrass him further, but from what I gather he told a few untruths to Laurie in order to get an appointment and then when he finally got into my home he interrogated me for 5½ hours. There's no other word for it. I felt as if I was on trial in my own sitting room. It was quite obvious that he wanted to do a hatchet job.

'I put it to you . . .' he kept saying as if he was Perry Mason, until in the end my head was spinning. Nothing I had to say seemed to satisfy him.

I have to expect this sort of thing I know. It's sad but true that as soon as you start getting nice things written about you in the paper, other papers want to write nasty things simply to make a change. I know this and yet it still hurts when they do it. It's very hard to ignore.

Worst of all was that 5½ hour grilling. I don't know whether I'm getting old or whether it's the effect of my stroke, but afterwards I felt exhausted and rather sick.

As it happened the story was so full of inaccuracies when it came out that you couldn't take it seriously but I'm grateful to that young man for one thing. He pointed out an error in my first book, *Voices In My Ear*, which I can now put right. Somehow the gremlins got into the works while the books were being put together and I've described a bombing raid in Grantham as happening in 1945, when in fact it happened several years earlier. Sorry about that. Looking back forty years things got out of sequence and my apologies to any readers who were misled.

Anyway suffice it to say that by the time the Barbican demonstration came round I was feeling rather depressed. It's a chilling sensation to know that people bear you ill will and want to believe the worst of you. Nevertheless I was determined not to let the readers down, so I got myself dolled up, pinned a smile on my face and set off for the concert hall.

We didn't get off to a good start.

'You can't park there,' said the security guard as we sat outside the posh doors of this space age building while the driver went to enquire where we were to go.

'We won't be a minute,' I said, 'the driver's just gone to find out the way to the concert hall.'

'Sorry madam, you can't wait there,' he repeated impatiently.

'Well there's nothing we can do about it because the driver's got the car keys,' I said.

Exasperated the guard moved away and a moment later the driver returned.

'Right Doris we go through here to the lift and that should take us right up to the concert hall.'

He opened the door, John got out and turned to help me because I get tangled up in my long theatre dresses if I'm not careful, when the security guard came running.

'Come on now move this car!' he insisted angrily.

The driver tried to argue, but it was no use. I could see that unless the car was moved we'd all end up in the police station.

'Go on, don't worry about us,' I said to the driver. 'We'll find it.'

So the car rolled away and John and I went into the plush building. It was an interesting place, no doubt about that. Huge and very modern with lots of light polished wood and little staircases that went up and down all over the place. Fortunately we were early, because John and I blundered about getting nowhere until at last one of the attendants took pity on us.

'We're looking for the concert hall,' I explained.

'Follow me,' she said.

Well I don't know what we'd have done without her — probably still been there looking for the lift I reckon. She led us up and down some more staircases and through a white walled corridor where there was some kind of arty exhibition going on. It was to do with different sounds I think because there were all these weird objects that produced different notes when struck. There was a rope ladder with hollow wooden rungs down which children dragged plastic sticks; there was a dangling thing twanging round a copper bowl; there were strips of metal that revolved and shook; and a pair of symbols that were very popular with the kids. The din was indescribable and we hurried through as fast as we could.

The attendant deposited us at the lift.

'You want the second floor,' she said.

So up we went and once again found ourselves in a long corridor looking bewildered. What people must have thought of me in my long dress and gold slippers at 2.00 in the afternoon I can't imagine.

Once again an attendant came to our rescue.

'We're looking for the concert hall,' I repeated weakly.

I was just beginning to think that it was all a joke and that the concert hall didn't exist, when the man opened a door on a scene of frantic activity.

Rows of seats led down to a large stage where Laurie and his helpers were rushing round laying carpet, setting out flowers and arranging chairs.

'Hello Doris,' said Laurie cheerfully. 'It's going to look wonderful.'

But it wasn't the glorious flowers that caught my eye, it was the stage. There were no curtains, no wings for me to stand in while waiting to go on, just rows and rows of seats sweeping right the way round. There was nowhere to hide, just this huge brand new stage of softly gleaming pale wood. It frightened the life out of me.

'This chap will take you to the dressing-room,' Laurie continued as if nothing was wrong. 'You've got plenty of time for a cup of tea.'

If I was the type to take tranquilisers, I'd have swallowed a handful then, but I'm not, of course. Instead I made do with a very strong cup of tea.

John was just putting the kettle on for another cup when the door opened and a hot and bothered Tony Ortzen almost fell into the room.

'I thought I'd never get here!' he gasped. 'I've been walking around this building for miles following the yellow lines. Follow the yellow lines, the notice says, but when you do you end up where you started!'

Tony was another candidate for a strong cup of tea.

'Tony, we've got to think about this,' I said when he was more relaxed. Tony was chairman for the afternoon and would be preceding me on stage to do the introductions.

'There are no wings for me to stand in, and I can't wait outside the door because it's made of glass and they'll see me through it, so we'll have to go on together.'

It meant rearranging his lines slightly, but Tony agreed it was the only way to do it.

By now I was feeling a nervous wreck. I made my escape to the loo as I always do when I want a bit of peace and quiet and silently I implored the spirit world for help.

'Ramanov, I badly need your help this afternoon,' I said.

Instantly there came a name. 'Craig,' said a distant voice.

'Craig hang on a minute,' I called, 'give me a bit more to go with it. Who are you looking for?'

'Shirley,' said the voice moving closer, and then, 'Wood.'

It wasn't much but it was enough to get me started.

'Okay Tony, I'm ready now,' I said when I came out, and so, bracing ourselves to face that daunting open stage, we went out.

Tony went through the glass doors and I was at his heels and as I crossed the threshold the whole place went up. They couldn't have given me a warmer welcome. Relaxing now I followed Tony up the steps to the stage and then I sat next to him while he made his modified introduction.

Right from the beginning everything went well.

'Just before I came on I heard a young boy called Craig,' I said, 'and he's looking for Shirley Wood. Is there anyone called Shirley Wood here?'

A woman came hurrying to the microphone. 'My name's Shirley, but not Wood,' she said.

'Do you know Craig?'

'Oh yes.'

'Listen Doris,' said Craig moving in closer, 'I didn't say Wood, I said Woodland. It's an address. Oh and I'm sixteen.'

Shirley confirmed that this was true and that she lived in Woodland Way.

'She's got my hair in a locket you know,' Craig told me proudly.

124

'Well what happened to you, lovey?' I asked him, 'Were you killed?'

'No, I had leukaemia,' said Craig, 'the last two or three years were pretty dreadful.'

'Yes they were,' said Shirley.

Craig mentioned his friends John and Thomas and his aunts Lily and Margaret and he wanted to wish his father happy birthday.

'My father is really my stepfather,' he confided, 'but I love him more than anything else in the world. I used to get a bit upset at times and Dad used to calm me down.'

Then he added, 'Dad's got my watch on you know.'

Out in the audience a man nodded.

'Yes he has,' said Shirley.

Craig tried to give me his dad's name. It was very short, only three letters, but I couldn't catch it properly.

'Three letters,' I said slowly, 'Roy, Ray . . .'

'Ray,' said Shirley.

'That's his dad.'

'Yes.'

Craig was delighted to have made contact so quickly. 'Dad didn't want to come because he didn't believe in this,' he laughed. 'He'll have to now, won't he?'

Not long after Craig had moved on, we had another satisfied visitor from the spirit world. I heard a woman's voice and the name Edie.

'I'm looking for my husband Norman, dear,' she told me. 'Oh and I drowned.'

I repeated this to the audience and suddenly near the back of the hall I became aware of a man struggling to his feet.

'Yes, that's Norman,' said his wife, 'but do watch

125

him on those steps. He's not very good on his legs and he doesn't see very well.'

'Yes that's true,' Norman agreed as he picked his way carefully down the aisle.

'Well take your time, love,' I told him. 'Your wife doesn't want you to hurt yourself.'

When Norman finally made it to the microphone he explained that I'd got his wife's name wrong:

'It's not Edie, it's Ethel,' he said.

Normally I'd have wondered if I'd got the wrong contact but in this case, since all the other details were correct, I knew that the mistake was mine.

'Sorry, love,' I apologised to Ethel, 'I thought you said your name was Edie.'

Ethel didn't care, she had more important matters on her mind.

'I'm worried about Norman because he's blaming himself,' she told me. 'He didn't hear me go but there was nothing he could have done. I got up at 2.00 in the morning when he was fast asleep. I'd been ill you see and I thought I had cancer. I didn't want to be a burden on him.'

'Yes she was afraid she had cancer of the bladder,' said Norman.

Ethel, who'd been married to Norman for forty years, walked miles until she came to some water, I think it was a river and then, confused and tired by the exertion, she slipped in and drowned.

'But he's still blaming himself and he mustn't,' she said. 'There was nothing he could have done. If I hadn't gone out that night I'd have gone another night.'

On a happier note she wanted Norman to know that she was still close and kept an eye on him just as she always did.

'He's put up clean curtains, just as I always used to at this time of the year,' she said. 'He carries my wedding ring in his pocket and he's moved into a one-room flat now. Oh yes and he's got my picture on his bedside table and every night before he goes to sleep he kisses it and I kiss him back.'

There was so much information coming through that Norman, who'd hardly got over the surprise at hearing his name called, couldn't take it all in.

At one point Ethel mentioned some friends of hers but Norman said he'd never heard of them.

'He has, he has,' said Ethel impatiently. 'He knows them as well as I do. They were in the old people's flats where we used to live.'

Light dawned when I mentioned the flats to Norman.

'Oh yes of course,' he said. 'They were Ethel's best friends there. I remember now.'

It was a marvellous contact and a touching display of the love between two elderly people. They'd had their ups and downs throughout forty years of marriage but they still loved each other as devotedly as they did on their wedding day. It was clear that Ethel was going to stay by Norman's side until the moment they were reunited in the spirit world.

The second half of the demonstration went just as well with many amusing little incidents to lighten the atmosphere. Earlier in the evening I'd heard the name Sandy repeated now and then and I'd taken it to be a shortening of Sandra. Nothing else came with it though and I didn't follow it up. Back in the dressing-room during the interval however, I got it again, but much more distinctly.

'It's not Sandy for Sandra,' said a Scottish and very male voice, 'It's Sandy for Alexander. I hope you can find my wife. I'm a bit reserved but I was determined to get through because she's come a long way.'

So after the break I asked for Sandy's wife and a neat Scottish lady with a dry sense of humour came forward.

First she confirmed the details. Yes, her husband Alexander had died of cancer in the neck, and yes, the illness only lasted twelve weeks.

But then Sandy mentioned Sarah.

'His mother,' sniffed Sandy's wife.

'They didn't get on very well,' said Sandy.

'No,' agreed his wife, 'she was an old vagabond.'

'Well he wants you to know love, that Sarah's here with him,' I put in.

'God help him,' said his wife tartly and there were roars of laughter from the audience.

Then Sandy asked for some flowers for his wife.

'Oh good,' she said when I told her, 'because he never gave me any when he was here.'

'Well I thought I'd better ask or she'd give me hell when she comes over,' Sandy confided. 'She's plagued with her back in the winter you know.'

'I'm plagued with it now,' added his wife.

But Sandy was obviously looking at the flowers piled up on the stage and choosing something nice.

'Could you give her one of the bouquets,' he asked, 'and could you give that big centre piece to the bairn's mother back there.'

Behind his wife at the microphone a young woman who'd lost a child waited for her turn.

'He says the bairn's mother behind you should have the big centre piece,' I said.

'He would,' said Sandy's wife, 'he's not paying for it.'

By now the audience were in stitches, but for all the

128

unsentimental exchanges there were tears in that woman's eyes and there was a great deal of affection between the couple.

The afternoon raced by and all too soon Tony Ortzen had to bring the demonstration to an end because there was another function taking place later that evening.

I left the stage to the most tremendous applause and people rushed forward to thank me for their messages, shake my hand or ask for autographs.

It really had been the most marvellous occasion

But I wasn't quite over the hurt caused by that newspaper reporter. The unpleasant article came out the day before a demonstration at Lewisham, and I was worried to think that people would believe the ugly things that were printed. Now I've got to prove myself all over again I thought sadly.

'Don't worry about it, love,' said John. 'Just do your work and you can't go wrong.'

But my work can be affected by my mental state and if I wasn't careful I knew I could make a hash of things just when I most wanted to do well.

I was pretty nervous by the time I got on stage but fortunately the first contact was marvellous.

'We sent you some flowers,' a man kept whispering in my ear, but I couldn't understand it because there were no flowers in the dressing-room.

It turned out that a beautiful bouquet signed just Lillian and John which had arrived at home some time before was from this man and his wife. I'd been puzzled at the time because there was no accompanying letter and I didn't know any Lillian and John. I assumed I must have given them a message at a theatre some time before and that the flowers were a thank you gift.

It didn't occur to me that the gift was a thank you in advance!

Well the man talking to me was John and he was looking for his wife Lillian. What's more he'd only passed the previous Thursday and they hadn't had the funeral yet.

John wasn't lonely on the other side. He'd met several workmates who'd gone over before him.

'But it wasn't right, Doris,' he told me. 'I wasn't an old man, I was only sixty-three.'

'Actually he was sixty-four,' said his wife. 'He was just sixty-four but he had his birthday while he was in hospital and he refused to celebrate it until he was home.'

'She hasn't washed my pyjamas yet,' said John. 'Silly really. She thinks she'll wash me away if she washes them but she won't because I'm there with her all the time.'

John went chattering on. He told me he'd left £53 in a drawer at home, that he'd pinched his wife from another fellow before they were married, and he even mentioned the budgie Bobby.

I couldn't have wished for a better way to start the evening, but for some reason instead of making me relaxed, it made me worry that I couldn't keep the quality going. Anxious thoughts crept in and the rest of the first half was dreadful. I was hearing things well enough but nothing came together. I got scraps of information all over the place and no one claimed them. I kept hearing something about a pub called The Golden Fleece, and some time-sharing appartments in Spain. But the messages didn't belong to each other and I got myself into a mess.

It's not working I thought in despair.

I went off at the intermission and had a cup of tea

and then I went to the loo and had a few tears. What's the matter with you girl? I asked myself sternly. God's on your side. Go out there and show them.

The little pep talk did the trick. Back I went and the second half went like a dream. All the bits and pieces that were such a jumble in the first half fell into place. We found the owner of the time-share appartment who had a message from his wife, we found the reference to the Golden Fleece pub — it turned out that the man who worked there had gone into the gents and killed himself. He'd only been married five months.

And so it went on. By the time I finished, the audience gave me a standing ovation and I came off walking on air.

'Don't let them bother you, Doris,' people kept telling me as I made my way back to the dressing-room. 'We don't believe a word of it. To hell with them, we love you.'

All my worries dissolved. Once again the spirit world had proved that I was wrong to doubt.

'Just trust in us and we won't let you down,' Ramanov was always telling me and sure enough they'd done it again!

Not long after this I received two lovely poems inspired by that article.

Why oh why, won't they see, when I've
    tried so hard to just be me,
I can't perform miracles, this I can't do
All that I've done is try to help you.
The messages come and in my own way,
I just pass on what your loved ones say,
I don't invent, I don't pretend, I just
    try to help as would any friend,
And if in the end some comfort I give, is

that so wrong if I help others to live
In the knowledge that somewhere in God's own
good time
Reunited they'll be in a joy so sublime,
If this I can do then happy I'll be,
Please don't condemn, I'm only me!

Sylvia Mallett dashed that off almost as soon as she heard of the attacks on my good name and shortly afterwards, John Wheeler of Sussex wrote this *Letter to Doris* in verse:

Few they are who have the Faith
To run the race and hold the pace,
When hard the track that they must run;
While others seem to have the fun.
Some fail by doubt and some by fear
And others when they've come so near
The winning post in psychic quest
Fail only through a lack of zest.
No sticks or stones can bar the way,
Nor even what the sceptics say ...
For those who run the race for truth
Eventually they find the proof.
Hold true to purpose and intent —
For steadfast faith will circumvent
The words of those who scoff and scorn
They are but young Souls newly born.
The lessons of successive life
The effort made, the stress and strife,
Will teach to everyone in turn
The lessons they are here to learn.
Then on that day to Heaven's pleasure,
A knowledge that each one will treasure,

That those who've run the race and won
Are helping now, we who still run.
For on the other side of death,
Running with unceasing zest
Are the keepers of the portals
The gateway twixt passed souls and mortals.

How could I possibly feel downhearted, with such
good friends as these?

Chapter Eight

Some years ago when I was in Australia, I happened to appear on the same TV programme as the pop singer Meat Loaf. Now I'm not very well up on pop singers and I was astonished as I was leaving the green room to see this young man walking in. Dressed all in black motorcycle leathers, he was one of the largest men I've ever seen. He was enormous.

'How on earth does he do all the jumping around that pop singers do at that size?' I whispered to one of the TV people as he led me to the set.

'Well I've heard they give him a whiff of oxygen before he goes on, then he does a number, comes off, they give him another whiff of oxygen and throw him back on again!'

It seemed incredible to me if it was true.

Anyway, without the benefit of oxygen myself, I went on, started to do a demonstration for the audience and the whole thing went so well that I ended up staying an hour!

Poor old Meat Loaf was waiting all that time for his entrance and as I came off he said, a little crossly I thought, 'Who *is* that old lady?'

'I might be an old lady, love,' I told him jokingly, 'but they've never had to give me oxygen yet!'

Meat Loaf laughed, the tension evaporated and suddenly we were friends.

Since then I've found that no matter how strange young people might look to my eyes, underneath the peculiar clothes and weird make-up, they are nearly always lovely people. I've had punks queuing at the stage door just to hand me a rose and the most bizarre looking reporters from young magazines writing beautiful articles full of spiritual understanding, about my work. It just shows that you can't judge people by their appearance.

Sadly though although a lot of pop singers are very nice people they do seem to get themselves into awful messes, and end up passing over long before their time. I've spoken to so many of them on the other side and it seems such a shame that so much talent is cut off in its prime.

One of the most famous stars I've 'met' in this way is Elvis Presley and not long ago I had a chance to renew our acquaintance. I must stress that I can't call up whoever I choose for a cosy chat. I mean I'd quite like a few words with Winston Churchill but why on earth should he want to talk to me? My only chance of contacting the great man is through a sitting with a member of his family or a friend, or if there was some sort of link.

In the case of Elvis Presley there was already a link because I'd spoken to him some years ago during a sitting for Marc Bolan's mother Phyllis. Marc was telling his mother about his new life on the other side and the friends he'd made. He was particularly thrilled to have met his idol Elvis Presley and he brought him

135

along to say hello. Marc introduced Elvis to his mother and Elvis introduced Marc to *his* mother who was with him on the other side. I recall that Elvis was a softly spoken young man and he seemed to be very polite. He kept calling me ma'am.

Anyway it was a pleasant interlude but I thought no more about it until the *Sun* newspaper rang me and asked if it was possible to contact Elvis. Apparently his wife Priscilla had just written a sensational book about their marriage and they wanted to know what Elvis thought of it. Would he like to defend his reputation from these slurs?

I was staying in Brighton at the time because I was doing a few theatre demonstrations and I knew I had a morning to spare.

'Well look I can't guarantee anything,' I said, 'I do know Elvis slightly but I've no idea whether he'll want to come and talk to me or not.'

The *Sun* said that they quite understood but they'd like to try all the same, so reporter Ruth Brotherhood was despatched to Brighton.

She arrived armed with an Elvis album and a wedding picture of Elvis and Priscilla, to help get me in the mood. I looked at the photograph. The couple were so young and eager looking, an apparently well matched pair. Both attractive and healthy, they should have had years ahead of them to live happily and raise a family. What a shame it had ended in bitterness and tragedy.

The hotel was right on the seafront but outside the traffic thundered by, as noisy as on any London street. Laurie closed all the windows to help me concentrate and then keeping that haunting photograph in my mind, I tuned in.

I took a while to make contact because there was no love link, but eventually I realised that a man was standing close by. As I homed in on the light that suddenly appeared in the room, I felt a tide of bewilderment and confusion washing around me. It was a sensation I was becoming used to. So many young people I contact these days carry the same muddled feelings with them, but this man seemed more mixed-up than most. Or at least he used to be when he was on the earth.

Then he spoke and I recognised the slow, southern voice and the quaint good manners.

'Yes it's me, ma'am,' he told me.

'Well Elvis,' I said silently, 'I expect you know what's been going on? So what's all this about you and your wife? Why's she been saying these things about you?'

There was a pause as if Elvis was trying to get his thoughts in order and then it all came tumbling out, a bit disjointed, but then he obviously found it difficult to put his feelings into words.

'I was brought up to treat women with reverence,' he said, 'I wanted my wife to be a virgin. That's why I chose Priscilla. I chose her from the beginning and I groomed her.'

He had clearly been a conceited man, and though he was struggling now to achieve humility it didn't come easily to him. Yet he loved Cilla, he truly loved her, he kept saying and I believed him.

'I made a great many mistakes in my life but the biggest mistake I ever made was with Priscilla. I put her on a pedestal. I treated her as something ... maybe I was a bit weird, but as something holy ... I had a very religious upbringing you see. I revered my mother and then I revered my wife and that was where I went wrong. She needed me to be a husband, a friend, and a lover — and I wasn't.'

137

But for a religious person he had some strange tastes. Suddenly his voice stopped and he showed me a picture. I was looking at a terrific-sized room and everything was black. Black, black, black everywhere, carpet, sheets, everything just black and huge mirrors reflecting it. In the mirrors I could see a bed, yet somehow I knew that this wasn't Cilla's bed. It was Elvis' private room.

'Well they did sleep separately later on,' Ruth explained.

Then the picture vanished and I was looking at another room — the bathroom. The contrast between the bathroom and the bedroom couldn't have been greater. Where the bedroom was all stark and black the bathroom was all pale marble and furs scattered across the floor.

'Sometimes I could be mean in spirit to my wife,' Elvis went on, sounding genuinely sorry. 'But does my daughter realise that when I used to lock myself away for days, that I loved her very much. It's just that I needed to take pills. I'm a hypochondriac I suppose. I used to take drugs for this, drugs for that. I was so frightened. I thought I had cancer. I passed blood sometimes.'

'Does he remember the early days with Priscilla?' asked Ruth because things were beginning to take a morbid turn.

Elvis's voice softened, 'She was only fourteen, just a school girl. I remember her in white. But I thought I was God Almighty. I thought I could take her and mould her. And I did. She was overawed by me. I really thought I was the king. And now I'm over here and I realise that I'm just an ordinary boy with a special gift of making music.'

Looking back over his life he could see the mess

he'd made of things and he was full of remorse.

'Forty-two. I was only forty-two,' he said. 'Oh God. I had all that money. What was the use of it? ... And what upset me was the rows afterwards. Colonel Parker, Vernon — there was plenty for everybody. Why row?'

As to Priscilla's revelations he wasn't worried for himself.

'It doesn't hurt me none,' he said. 'But what about Lisa. Will it hurt Lisa, I'd like you to ask Cilla that. It doesn't hurt me none, I'm out of it aren't I, but why hurt Lisa. She doesn't need the money. Why do it?'

'Yes, but what went wrong, love?' I asked. 'Cilla loved you at first. What happened?'

There was a long silence. I got the impression that Elvis didn't like admitting to his faults.

'When I should have been doing my duty as a husband I was shut up reading the Bible,' he said.

'There must have been more to it than that, love.'

There was another pause.

'I was wrong wrong wrong wrong wrong,' he suddenly burst out passionately. 'After she'd had the baby I thought she was sullied. I confused her with my mother. It was like making love to my mother. I couldn't do it.'

He seemed so upset, I changed the subject and asked him about the people he'd met on the other side. I knew his mother was with him of course but he mentioned that his father Vernon had since joined them and several other names that Ruth couldn't place. He talked of Betsy and Herbert, someone called Mary Ann, or Marian, and also of a preacher. He kept on about this preacher as if the man had had some kind of special significance for him.

It was clear that he was a very weird man in his

personal life. Half of him wanted to let rip and go with tarts, but the religious part of his nature held him back. As a compromise by all accounts it seems he liked his wife to dress up in a tarty way to act out his fantasies.

'I thought I was her master,' said Elvis, 'I took her from nothing and I thought she should be grateful. I was wrong . . .'

He had learned a lot since his passing, yet he hadn't quite managed to rid himself of self pity. He knew that he became bloated and grotesque in his last years and yet he was inclined to blame everybody but himself.

'Why couldn't I have met somebody who could have straightened me out?' he asked, his voice rising to a childish whine.

I'm afraid I lost patience a bit with that.

'Everyone gets under pressure you know love and they have to work it out for themselves,' I said rather more sharply than I intended.

Elvis crumbled immediately. 'I know I must have been weak. I wanted to be mothered. I wanted my wife to be my mother and the other half of me wanted to be the master. I was a coward too. I couldn't have borne a painful passing. I couldn't stand that. My mother died a painful death and I couldn't bear it to happen to me. . . .'

'D'you mean you took yourself over because you were afraid you had cancer?' I asked him silently because it almost sounded as if he was telling me that his death had been a suicide.

He shook his head vehemently.

'I didn't mean to do it. I got mixed up. I took a lot of pills but I didn't mean to do it. . . .'

An impression of his last moments swept over me. I was on the bathroom down on my knees on the fur rug. I was saying my prayers I think, then I felt very sick and there was a terrible pain in my head.

He kept saying something about his toes being black which I couldn't fathom at all.

'D'you mean you had black socks on? Or that you didn't have socks on?' I asked, but the reply was jumbled and I couldn't make it out.

'My mother came for me, ma'am,' he added, 'and I went before my father.'

There was a pause and I gathered that he wasn't best pleased with his father. He seemed to think there had been squabbles over money and he was annoyed that his father had married again. He didn't think he should have replaced Elvis' beloved mother.

On the subject of his daughter Lisa, though, his feelings were plain.

'I'm very proud of her. She's beginning to look like me. I want her to be happy. Tell her to be careful. Tell her to make sure she marries a man who loves her for herself and not for her money.'

He paused, 'I want her to have a normal life and have babies. In fact I'm going to have three grand-children ...'

The power was getting very weak by this time. It had been a long and emotional sitting and I was exhausted. I think Elvis was finding it a struggle too.

'Well I think we'll have to stop now,' I told Ruth, 'I can hardly hear him.'

But even as I spoke I heard one last sentence floating towards me before the vibrations went dead.

'Please ask my wife to forgive me. ...'

I felt quite shaken when the sitting was over. What an unhappy man Elvis Presley had been. I thought of all the people who must have envied him his talent, his early good looks, his money and fame. To think he had all those things and yet he had nothing ... What a terrible, terrible waste.

Chapter Nine

The policewoman looked stern. She'd walked into the party in her severe navy uniform, her hat pulled down low on her forehead and everything had gone quiet. Conversation stopped, the music trailed away and guests watched her uneasily from the corners of their eyes.

'Is there a John Stokes here?' she asked crisply, unconcerned about the effect she was having on the party.

John walked forward, 'Yes love. That's me.'

'John Stokes I've got a warrant for your arrest,' she told him.

Anyone else might have been worried, but John, secure in the knowledge that he couldn't possibly have done anything wrong, was not alarmed. He knew there must be some mistake.

'Oh really,' he said, 'what for?'

'I believe you have a dog?'

'Yes. Boots.'

'Have you got a licence?'

John frowned, 'No, I don't think so, he's not a year

old yet. We don't need a licence do we?'

The policewoman took out her notebook.

'I'll have to take down your particulars.'

'All right,' said John, 'what do you want to know?'

She paused, a mischievous grin warming her face.

'Would you like to unbutton my shirt?'

At this point I couldn't control myself any longer and I burst out laughing. The 'policewoman' was a Kissogram I'd organised as an extra present for John on our 42nd wedding anniversary. What's good enough for the executives in London is good enough for my husband I thought and I wanted him to have a really memorable occasion.

To the amazement of the guests, the policewoman slowly peeled off her formal uniform to reveal a leopard-skin leotard, stockings and suspender belt underneath. It was all quite tasteful. There were no rude boobs or anything like that, and John didn't turn a hair. At the end the girl said.

'I have to post the telegram, John,' and she pulled out his trousers and stuck the telegram down the front.

'John wants everyone to play Postman Pat!' shouted a joker amongst the guests and everyone fell about laughing.

It was a marvellous party.

In fact we had two marvellous parties in January. The first to celebrate my 66th birthday and the second, our anniversary, which falls in the same month.

We'd not had a party for years and as my birthday approached I started thinking how nice it would be to have a really good do. The problem was, where? Spacious as our semi seems to us after the small ex-serviceman's flat where we used to live, it's still not large enough to hold all our friends — not if they want to breathe as well that is!

'Well what about the pub?' said Laurie when I mentioned the problem.

As well as looking after me, Laurie also runs a pub in the East End.

'The saloon bar's quite nice and it would certainly be big enough,' he said.

So it was settled. Iris, Laurie's wife, did all the catering; she laid on a magnificent spread. Brendan Blake, an old friend who is also a professional singer and comedian, led the entertainment and we had a real old knees-up. Derek Jameson, another old friend, came along and afterwards he wrote in the paper, 'Top medium Doris Stokes doesn't go to posh restaurants on her birthday — she celebrates in an East End pub!'

Well really, what would I want with a posh restaurant at my age? I'm not out to impress anybody. It was much more fun in the pub. We had a terrific time and people enjoyed themselves so much they said: 'When can we have another one?'

So we did it all over again on our wedding anniversary.

Patrick brought his old grandmother who is ninety-seven to the second party and everyone made a fuss of her. She came along dressed up to the eyes in her little fur coat, and Brendan Blake sang 'When Irish Eyes Are Smiling' specially for her. He had to sing right in her ear because she's rather deaf these days, but she loved it and ninety-seven or not she was up on the floor dancing away with the rest of us.

I have to admit that even though I've been complaining of shaky legs ever since my stroke, I felt as if I could dance all night. It was wonderful.

With the anniversary approaching it seemed a good time to tackle John again on the subject of a new wedding ring. When we were married John bought me a 29s 11d utility ring because the cheap utility rings were all you could get in those days — unless you were a millionaire I suppose.

Well it wasn't very good quality. Over the years it grew thinner and thinner and on our 30th anniversary I asked John if he'd buy me a new one.

He wouldn't.

'No,' he said, 'it's not the money. I'll buy you anything else but I want you to keep the ring you were married in.'

It was sweet and sentimental and I was rather touched so I kept the ring on my finger and settled for something else. But the next twelve years took their toll. The ring became so thin and sharp it kept cutting my finger. I was forever taking it off, putting on a plaster and replacing the ring when my finger was healed, only for it to cut my finger all over again.

'It's no good John,' I said at last, 'I'll have to have a decent wedding ring. I can't go on like this. I'll have a septic finger.'

So reluctantly John agreed to buy me a new ring, and I chose a beautiful model of intertwined red and white gold leaves. Even John had to admit it was gorgeous. We put the old ring away in a box and I made sure John made a note of where it was kept.

'If I go before you, John,' I told him, 'for goodness sake don't forget to take the good ring off and put the other one on before you cremate me!'

All in all the early part of the year was a very sociable time. I was highly excited to be invited to Hatchards, the exclusive bookshop in Piccadilly, for their Author of the Year reception.

As it happened I was suffering from the remnants of a cold and I'd been left with a sore throat and an irritating cough every time I opened my mouth. I didn't dare have anything to eat in case it set me off and I only stayed half an hour but it was fun all the same.

It was very posh indeed. There was a toastmaster in red coat and white gloves to announce you as you walked in. There were cameras everywhere to photograph your entrance and there were so many famous authors it made your head spin. After Dick Francis, Dulcie Grey, Jilly Cooper and Jeffrey Archer, I lost count.

Jeffrey Archer was very nice. I was sitting there sipping my orange juice and watching the dazzling crowd when he came over and sat on the floor at my feet.

'I'm kneeling in front of a superstar!' he said with the most charming smile.

I was amazed. I'd always thought he would be a bit of a stuffed shirt but he wasn't at all. I wouldn't be surprised if he went back into politics seriously and ended up Prime Minister one day!

At the risk of sounding as if I trip over stars every day of the week I must also mention my visit to Thames TV for *An Audience With Billy Connolly*. I was invited to be part of the audience for the television show and I enjoyed it very much.

Billy Connolly was a little bit strong in places, for me, but for all that he drew on his experiences as a child and I found I could identify with him. He talked of the way you had coats piled on the bed in winter because there weren't enough blankets to go round, and the way everything was poshed up when the vicar dropped in and the best biscuits, kept for special occasions, were brought out.

It brought back a lot of memories. We were taught as children that the vicar or priest was something special and everything had to be the best for him. I remember long afterwards when I was staying with friends in Dublin, being very surprised at the amount of whisky the priest put back when he dropped in on Friday evenings. But then I thought, why am I surprised just because he's wearing a dog collar? He's still a man and he has his weaknesses like everyone else.

It was just the way I was brought up. We were taught that the vicar was above the rest of us. We were very poor, yet we weren't miserable. I remember going round to Maggie Roberts' father's corner shop for a halfpenny worth of broken biscuits. It didn't bother me because it seemed quite normal. I didn't know anyone who bought biscuits any other way.

Maggie Roberts of course went on to be Prime Minister Margaret Thatcher, but in those days she was just Maggie from the shop, a smart little girl who always did her homework. Her father was a preacher too and on Sunday nights we kids got a poke of sweets if we sat through his sermons at the chapel. We sat there for hours letting all this hellfire and damnation wash over our heads, so that we could claim our sweets at the end of it!

Oh yes, Billy brought it all back. After the show we stayed for supper and Billy came over to say hello.

'Even if I couldn't have seen your face I would have known where you were,' he said, 'because you gave off a glow.'

'Well it surely wasn't my jewellery, love!' I joked, but inside I was touched. What a lovely compliment.

But if I've given the impression that I'm leading a wild life of parties and shows I must explain that these things are just the fun highlights and between them there's been a great deal of solid, hard work.

When I'm not making theatre appearances, Laurie keeps me busy with a steady stream of personal sittings. They're all booked through his office and I never know who's coming until they arrive. I'm very honoured to think that one of my recent sitters was Benazir Bhutto, daughter of the former Prime Minister of Pakistan who was hanged by the military regime. I saw her on television not long ago surrounded by a quarter of a million people — and to think that she sat there on the sofa in my sitting room, with me just in my old dressing gown. It's a strange world.

In fact Benazir almost didn't get a sitting. She'd been booked in for some time and I'd had to cancel the first appointment through ill health. By a stroke of bad luck I was ailing again when the second appointment came round and I asked Laurie to postpone the meeting once more. But this time he couldn't contact Benazir. So there I was resting in bed, when there was a knock at the door.

Dragging on my old dressing gown, I went down to find Benazir, her sister, and her friend Jane, all standing in the hall unaware that Laurie had been phoning all over London in an attempt to stop them coming.

'Oh dear, shall we go and leave you in peace?' asked Jane when they saw that I was obviously unwell.

But I couldn't turn them away once they'd come this far.

'No it's all right, love,' I said. 'Come and sit down and we'll have a try, but I feel so rotten I can't promise we'll get anything.'

John put the kettle on and the girls made themselves comfortable. Benazir seemed a very nice young woman. She was slim and dark with pale gold skin and heavy glasses that gave her the look of a young Nana Mouskouri.

148

She couldn't have been very old, little more than a child to me, and I had no idea as she sat there holding her cup with delicate fingers, that she wanted her father's advice because she had very big plans indeed. Despite the fact that politics had killed her father and her brother, Benazir was planning to return to Pakistan to take over where her father had left off.

It was her father himself who mentioned her plans. At first he talked of family matters. He mentioned his nicknames for Benazir and her sister: Pinky he called her, and her sister was known as Sunny. He also mentioned his first wife, his child wife he said, from Iran. He spoke of his son who had been poisoned, then he talked of the night he himself passed over.

'There were twelve of them,' he said. 'They came for me in the night and they strangled me.'

Whether he meant they strangled him in his cell, or whether he was referring to the fact that he was hanged wasn't clear. Most of all he wanted Benazir to know that she had his support and his blessing.

'Verdie,' he kept saying — that's the nearest I can get to the spelling. I thought it was a name.

'No,' said Benazir, 'in our language it means I promise.'

'I promise I'll always stand by you,' he said.

He told her that despite the opposition she would go back to Pakistan to a tumultuous welcome from the people and it was then that I realised what a brave girl this was.

'Get the people behind you,' he kept saying. 'It's the people who count. You can pick any monkey out of the jungle and stick him in a uniform and he'll think he rules the world, but the people will know. You can't fool the people.'

He went on to give Benazir the names of the people

she could trust and those she couldn't and he talked of papers locked away in a safe somewhere, that she might need.

It was a marvellous sitting and over and over he kept reminding her, 'I'll always stand by you. I promise.'

Afterwards as she rose to go a look of great determination came into her fine dark eyes. 'I'll do it, and I'll do it for my father,' said Benazir.

'No forget that, love,' I told her. 'Don't do it for your father. Do it for the people.'

Shortly afterwards I heard that Benazir, at great personal risk had returned to Pakistan where thousands upon thousands of people had turned out to greet her. I marvelled at her courage; that slip of a girl hoping to rule a country and now I follow her career with fascination. I just hope her dad's taking good care of her.

Shortly after Benazir's visit, a family from Finland came to see me. As I said before, Laurie never tells me anything about my sitters in advance so their stories are always a complete surprise to me as they unfold. But in this case I sensed great tragedy as soon as the family walked in.

It turned out that their teenage son and their nephew had died in separate incidents, both of which could have been regarded as suicide.

The couple's son, Karri, soon put me right about his passing.

'It was an accident, I didn't mean to do it,' he assured me. 'I was cleaning the gun and looking down the barrel when I tripped and it went off.'

Pira, his poor mother, had found him. Apparently the boy was very interested in chemistry and he wanted to be a pharmacist. He liked to carry out experiments in his bedroom and when she heard the bang, she thought something had exploded. She raced upstairs expecting to have to put out a fire. Instead she found her son slumped back on the bed with shotgun wounds.

The other boy, Petri, was just as tragic. His father was rather strict and he was worried about some exams that were coming up. Anyway, one day he went along for the ride while his father visited a sick friend in hospital. While his father was at the bedside, Petri took the lift to the top of the building and jumped off. Another friend who was with him, Kolevi, also jumped.

'It was the drugs,' said Kolevi, 'I honestly thought I could fly.'

Petri was very sad about the pain he'd caused his family.

'We were in Dad's Landrover,' he said. 'The last time he saw me alive I was sitting in the Landrover — the next I was lying dead at the foot of the building. I'm so sorry. I was depressed.'

There were a great many family details as well as these harrowing accounts, but most of all both boys wanted to get through to Pira's other son, Nicholas, who'd come with her.

'Don't get involved in drugs or anything,' they kept saying over and over again. 'Be a good boy Nicholas.'

Nicholas kept protesting that nothing was further from his mind, but they seemed so worried about him that it made me wonder.

In direct contrast to the warning mood of the Finnish sitting was the little girl who came back to her parents shortly afterwards. They'd hardly sat down when a little girl danced into the room, there was no other word for it, and said:

151

'Gay by name and gay by nature.'

'Now what does she mean by that?' I asked. 'Was her name Gay?'

'No it's our surname,' said her mother.

And the next moment the little girl gave me her Christian name. I thought she said Leonie, but it was Lianne.

Lianne had great vitality and she bubbled on without inhibition.

'I was crossing the road,' she told me, 'and I was ever so careful. I was on the zebra crossing when the car hit me. But I didn't feel anything.'

She chatted about her mother's new flat and the new car.

'But she hasn't seen it,' said her father incredulously.

'I have you know,' said Lianne indignantly.

She even mentioned Brian, the disc jockey who lived next door who sometimes put records on for her.

'I loved dancing,' she said, 'and I had a boyfriend called Terry.'

'Yes, little Terry Williams,' said her mum.

She was so eager not to miss anything that sometimes I had difficulty catching up with her and when this happened she got cross with me.

'I *am* impatient,' she admitted when I appealed to her to slow down a bit, 'I'm like me dad. He gets impatient.'

By the end of the sitting both parents were almost speechless.

'I didn't think it would be like this,' admitted Lianne's father at last. 'It was so different to what I'd expected.'

Like a lot of people he feared to find me in long flowing robes, ear-rings down to the shoulders and maybe a crystal ball for good measure, but of course it's not like that at all. I smile to myself as I watch their faces when they see my sunny sitting room, the mugs of coffee and me wandering about in my carpet slippers. I often feel it must be a great disappointment to them!

Not all spirit people are as easy to talk to as Lianne however. Sometimes they are still so indignant about what they consider to be their untimely passing, that the sheer force of their resentment blocks everything else out.

I felt particularly badly about this when I came up against the problem with a sitter from America. He'd come such a long way to get a message from his mother and when we finally got started she was so stifled with bitterness that other spirit people kept popping in with good wishes for the friend who'd come with him.

All I could learn from the mother was that she'd passed away during an operation. She kept touching me behind the ears to indicate where she'd been cut until in the end I realised that she'd been having a facelift.

'It needs looking into,' she said again and again. 'It shouldn't have happened. I shouldn't have come over here yet. I'm only sixty-one and I didn't even look sixty-one. They are saying my heart gave out. Nonsense. There was nothing the matter with my heart. It needs looking into. See a lawyer.'

She was a very forthright lady and she didn't mince her words but I couldn't get her to discuss anything else. She grudgingly showed me a brief picture of her house, a beautiful single storey place in a pale wash colour, set in a beautiful garden, but then she kept returning to the operation and the possible court case.

She was all for legal action, no doubt about that.

'I hate injustice,' she said, 'and this isn't right. It needs looking into.'

I could get practically nothing else from her and it was clear that I wouldn't for quite a while yet. Once she's accepted her fate and settled down on the other side the bitterness will clear, but until then there was nothing much I could do.

'I'm sorry love,' I told her poor son. 'She's making it so hard for me.'

And his friend was embarrassed too, about all the personal messages *he'd* received:

'I shouldn't have come, I've spoiled it for you,' he said apologetically.

'No, really, I don't mind,' the sitter told him gallantly. 'It's been fascinating to hear your messages.'

I felt dreadful but it couldn't be helped.

'Perhaps we can do better next time you come to England,' I promised.

But not all my sittings are conducted face to face with my sitters. Sometimes I have to work by telephone. Recently I even gave a radio interview, broadcast in Belfast, from the comfort of my own bed! This wasn't the height of laziness I hasten to add. I'd fully intended to go to the studios in London but unfortunately a tummy bug struck just as I was getting ready to leave.

I was up, washed and breakfasted. The car was waiting and I slipped upstairs to put my boots on because it was a cold morning. I bent over to pull on the right boot and suddenly my head swam, my breakfast came back and there was an intense pain in my stomach. Oh no, what's the matter now? I wondered. I went back, washed again, reapplied my makeup and ignoring my bendy legs, I went downstairs.

The driver was waiting in the hall.

'Come on Doris the traffic's building up,' he said. He helped me on with my coat, then he stopped.

'You can't go out like that, you're burning up.'

I put my hand to my cheek. Sweat was pouring down my face, yet I felt cold. John came out and felt my forehead.

'Yes, love, you've got a temperature. You can't go out like that. Go back to bed.'

So the electric blanket was switched on, I climbed thankfully back into bed and Laurie got the studios on the phone to break the news to them that I wouldn't be coming. They weren't pleased of course, but they managed to arrange a link-up with Belfast to my phone and I did the whole thing tucked up in bed!

But most of my phone work I'm happy to say is conducted from the armchair in my sitting room. A phone sitting can never take the place of a personal meeting of course, but sometimes the case is so urgent, I have to contact the people immediately. I can't give them much over the phone, but a few scraps at the right time can mean more than yards and yards of messages years after the event.

Not long ago I talked to a couple who'd written to me with a very distressing story. The previous Easter their little son had been given a small chocolate egg containing a model car. The egg was not recommended for children under three years of age, but their little boy was three and they couldn't imagine what danger could lurk in an innocent looking piece of confectionery.

The little boy tore off the foil wrapping, bit into the chocolate and then started to choke. The model car inside was in pieces, ready to be assembled, and the lad had swallowed a lump of plastic with his mouthful of chocolate. It lodged in his throat and no amount of slapping on the back would shift it.

The frantic parents rushed him to hospital but it was too late. Before the surgeon could operate, he was gone.

In fact at first, the parents didn't even want a sitting. They contacted me to ask if I could tell Esther Rantzen about the case. They were anxious to get the eggs banned from sale to prevent any more tragedies happening.

'We wouldn't want any other parents to have to go through what we've been through,' they said.

Laurie wrote to *That's Life* explaining what had happened and got a very nice letter back, thanking him for drawing the matter to their attention and saying that they were investigating the case. That was the last we heard and sadly it was too late to get the eggs banned for Easter 1986. But it wasn't the last we heard of the story. Not long afterwards Laurie had a phone call from the father of the little boy. It was now a year since his son's passing and his wife was taking it very badly. Could I possibly talk to her on the phone?

I couldn't refuse. Laurie gave me the number, which was in Ireland and I rang it immediately.

The poor couple were still very upset and a bit nervous but I was able to get their son quite quickly.

'Daddy's been painting,' he told me.

'Is he an artist, love?' I asked. 'Does he paint pictures?'

The boy laughed, 'No he's been painting the house.'

'Does it look nice?' I asked silently.

'Yep!' said the boy. Not yes, but yep.

His father was amazed. 'That's right. That's just what he used to say. It was always yep.'

The boy went on to talk a little more about his

family and what they were doing. He also mentioned the new car they'd recently bought.

By the end of the call the parents sounded dazed but happier and I could only hope that my few words had been of help.

I had a similar request a few weeks after this. A man whose handicapped son had passed unexpectedly just two or three *hours* before, phoned Laurie with a desperate appeal. His wife was expecting a baby and she was so distraught at the loss of her first child, that he feared for her and the unborn baby.

Apparently their much loved first child, Mark, was a bit of a handful and they were persuaded to put him into a home for a few days to give his mum a break while she had the baby.

Mark was cutting his back teeth at the time so when the home phoned shortly afterwards to say that he had a slight temperature, they weren't worried. But Mark's temperature did not respond to junior aspirin. He was sent to hospital and by the time the family found out the next day, he was dead.

It was a terrible shock to them. They'd accepted that he wouldn't have a long life, but they'd hoped they might have him for five or six years at least. Worse still was the way they'd discovered the news. They'd telephoned the hospital to find out what ward their son was in and were told he wasn't in a ward. He was in the morgue — he was dead.

It was a shocking blow.

'Please could Doris just speak to my wife?' the husband begged. 'She's in such a state we don't know what to do with her.'

How could anyone refuse such a plea? I telephoned immediately. The poor girl was sobbing uncontrollably at the end of the phone but I did my best. In such circumstances you can't do a lot because the grief has to come out but I hoped that a little reassurance got through.

I saw the little boy within seconds of tuning in even though he'd passed such a short time before. He was a dear little chap standing straight and firm on his own two legs. I knew he was handicapped but I didn't know in what way, until Mark showed me. He kept drawing my attention to his head which he held with great pride and he tilted his chin and put his head right back, so that he could look at the ceiling. Then he grinned triumphantly at me. He was obviously showing off a new ability and I guessed that he'd had no control over his head before.

'That's right,' said his mother, 'he had cerebral palsy. He couldn't hold his head up. It used to flop.'

'Well he can now, love,' I told her. 'He wants to emphasise that. He's all right now.'

Mark was too young to hold a conversation himself, so the people who were looking after him, his great grandmother I think it was, came to give a few family details. It was all rather difficult and confused, the contact blurred by the tremendous emotions coming from Mark's mum, but at the end, just before the power went, Mark came and put a blue and white teddy bear on my knee. This was the toy he wanted to take with him.

'Yes he loves that bear,' said his mother. 'I'll put it in his coffin with him.'

It was all very sad, but they seemed to find a little comfort in the news of their son.

Afterwards I received a beautiful letter from them thanking me for my time. Those few minutes on the phone had made all the difference to them, they said. Now they were trying to pick up the pieces of their lives in the knowledge that their little boy could run and play like other children in his new life on the other side.

Chapter Ten

The other day I was reading through my morning mail when one particular letter which had started quite normally suddenly made me choke on my eleven o'clock coffee. I was so angry I could hardly finish the page. It was from a distressed young mother whose baby daughter was stillborn. The poor girl had gone to a local medium in Shoreham, Essex hoping for some comfort and instead had been given some news that nearly made her take an overdose.

'You're being punished,' the medium told her. 'In a past life you abused children and so now you have to pay for what you did.'

The poor girl was in a terrible state wondering what on earth she could have done and how long her 'punishment' was going to last. Did this mean she'd never bear a healthy child?

Without further ado I dumped a whole lapful of letters on the floor and reached for the phone. The spirit world were right behind me in this because the girl had printed her phone number on the letter and when I dialled it she was in.

'Of course you're not being punished love,' I told her when I'd explained who I was. 'I've never heard such nonsense. God wouldn't do that. Your little girl is one of the special children who didn't need to stay on earth.'

I calmed her down and explained our philosophy as best I could.

'You go and have another baby, love, I'm sure it'll be all right this time,' I said. 'But listen this is important. Have you got the number of that medium who told you such wicked things? We've got to put a stop to this.'

'No I didn't keep it. I didn't want anything else to do with her,' she said, 'but I can find it. She advertises in the local paper every week.'

She went off and I heard the crackle of newspaper. Then she was back.

'Yes here it is Doris,' and she read me the number.

'I'm afraid she's not available,' said the man who answered the phone. 'Can I make an appointment for you?'

'No,' I said firmly. 'I'd just like to speak to her. My name is Doris Stokes.'

'Doris Stokes?' His voice changed, 'Well to be honest Doris she's in the bath at the moment. Just a minute I'll get her.'

It was 11.30 in the morning, an odd time to be having a bath but there you are. There was a long pause and then this 'medium' came to the phone.

'Did you tell a young woman who came to you after having a stillborn baby daughter that she was being punished?' I asked after introducing myself.

'Yes,' she said calmly.

The lack of remorse in her voice made me so angry I could hardly speak.

'Well I've lost four children, three before they were born. How d'you account for that?'

'You're being punished too,' she said. 'You both must have abused children in a previous life and you're working out your Karma.'

'Where on earth d'you get such ideas from? I've never heard such rubbish,' I spluttered.

But the woman was unshakeable.

'It's true,' she insisted. 'I'm not a spiritualist, I've broken away from that and followed my own ideas.'

'But don't you realise that the woman was on the point of taking herself over because of what you told her?'

The 'medium' at the other end of the phone sighed unrepentantly.

'I look on myself as a surgeon,' she said, 'a surgeon has to cut out the bad parts to make the rest well, and the operation hurts. It does hurt when you come to realise the wrong you've done in previous lives, but once you understand it you can start to put it right.'

'Do you really think God would allow a tiny child to go back to the spirit world before it was born simply because of the mother?' I asked, in a last vain hope that she would see sense.

'Yes,' she said.

It was hopeless. I couldn't get through to her. Either she genuinely believed what she was saying or she simply didn't care about the grief she was causing.

'Well I think it's disgusting,' I said angrily, 'and I don't think you're worthy to call yourself a medium.'

And I put the phone down.

But I couldn't let it rest there. I invited the young mother to my next demonstration and at Question Time she raised the subject in the form of a question so that I could reassure the whole audience that people are not punished in this life for things they'd done in previous lives.

Better still, while I was answering the question I suddenly heard one of the young woman's relatives speaking to me. Now normally I try not to go into sittings during Question Time because it's not fair to the rest of the audience who're waiting patiently for contacts, but on this occasion I broke my rule.

'They're telling me your child went back to the spirit world fifty minutes before she was born,' I said.

The young mother gasped.

'That's what they said at the hospital. They said she stopped breathing fifty minutes before she was still-born.'

I went on to tell her who was looking after the baby and a few more family details and she seemed much happier.

Afterwards I had a letter from her husband saying, 'You don't know what peace of mind you've given us. My wife was going through hell thinking it was her fault we lost our daughter.'

I was very pleased to have been able to help and even more pleased that we could have got the point across to so many people. That's the marvellous thing about Question Time, it gives everybody a chance to talk about the things that have been bothering them and people who are too shy to come forward often hear answers to questions they were too nervous to ask.

I thought you might like to see a cross-section of the sort of points that come up at Question Time:

Q. *What happens if there's a nuclear war?*
A. We'll all go over together love. It would probably be the end of this world but not the spirit world.

Q. *Is there any reason why your loved ones can't get a message through, no matter how hard you try to receive it? Is it a judgement?*

A. You need to be a medium to pick up messages and sometimes even a medium is not successful with everyone. The sitter has to be on the same wavelength as the medium.

Q. *My husband died at forty-two. If I live to be eighty will he be eighty when we meet?*

A. No. He'll be just as you want to see him and you will look younger too.

Q. *When my mentally handicapped son dies, will he be like it still and will he remember his life with us?*

A. Of course he'll remember his time with you and he'll lose his handicap. He is a soul that has chosen to come back like this to make you learn. I'll lay odds everyone loves him and that you've learned lots from him.
Yes we have.
You must be a wonderful person to have one of these special children. God only chooses the best.

Q. *If someone didn't believe in life after death when they were alive, can they get a message through when they've passed?*

A. Oh yes. He'll have found out now, won't he!

Q. *Will he be treated the same as those who believed?*

A. Of course he will.

Q. *When I pass over will my husband come for me?*

A. Yes, love, you will see him before you leave the earth plane. Nurses who've seen patients 'die' will tell you that they start talking to people who're not

164

there and this is often dismissed as 'rambling'. Not so. The patient has seen his spirit people who've come to help him over to the other side.

Q. *When someone wants to get in touch with you can you tell by his smell?*

A. Yes. When a man is present you might smell his favourite tobacco, when a woman is there you might smell the perfume she loved on the earth plane. This doesn't mean they still use it. It's simply a means of identification.
I can smell my father's after-shave.
He's obviously trying to let you know that he's close.

Q. *If someone commits suicide, how long is it before they can make contact through a medium?*

A. I've had them back the same day.

Q. *How many different planes are there?*

A. I don't really know love. I know there are very low planes where people like Hitler go. I also know that I won't be able to go where my children are because they knew no sin so they will be higher up than me. But this doesn't mean I won't see them. They can come and see me whenever they like.

Q. *Do they still cook on the other side? My nan used to love cooking and she made delicious oxtail soup. Will she still be able to do it over there?*

A. Well I expect she will if she wants to love, though I don't suppose it'll be necessary.

Q. *When you sit in a developing circle can two people be helped by one guide?*

A. No. Each one of us has our own spirit guide or teacher and that person has voluntarily given up their progression in the spirit world to come back to the earth plane with us. Even before your body is conceived your guide is with your spirit in the spirit world and when you go back to the spirit world the guide goes back.

We had a little dabble with a board and it said two of us had the same guide.

I wouldn't think so, love. I know my guide couldn't cope with two like me. It takes him all his time to keep me in order!

Q. *Why do some people suffer so much in the world while others come through unscathed?*

A. I think it's all to do with what we have to learn. I have learned a lot through suffering. Before I lost my baby I could meet people in the street and say, hello so and so, you don't look very well, and she would say, 'No, I lost my mother yesterday.' I'd say how sorry I was and I'd mean it but then I'd walk around the corner, see a dress shop and forget all about it as I looked at the dresses in the window. Yet once I'd had tragedy myself, my attitude changed. Now I suffer with people because I understand what they're going through.

Q. *Some people seem to get away with doing such bad things.*

A. Yes I know they do but they don't get away with it on the other side. Hitler will have to start at the bottom in a cold desolate place over there and until he shows remorse he won't rise. There *is* evil in the world. All we can do is try to brighten our own little corner.

Q. If you lose a baby through miscarriage does it meet up with your loved ones?

A. Not immediately. They wait till they're full term and then they are born into the spirit world and go to your relatives. Did you lose your baby at four months?
Yes.
Did you know it was a boy?
Yes.
Well they've called him Simon over there!

Q. I lost two children last year. Will they be together?

A. Yes.

Chapter Eleven

Practically every postbag these days brings me one or two beautiful poems along with the sad stories of tragedy and heartbreak. I save them up to enjoy when I've got a moment or two to spare and I must say the talent of perfectly ordinary people who've never written a poem before in their lives, never ceases to amaze me.

I can't possibly publish them all, there just isn't the space, but I thought you might like to see a selection of some of my favourites.

The first 'So Now You Know' was sent to me by George Gordon from Tyne and Wear. George didn't actually write the poem himself, apparently the author is unknown, but it so accurately portrays the way I feel half the time that I couldn't stop laughing.

So Now You Know
There's nothing the matter with me
I'm as healthy as can be
I've got arthritis in both knees
And when I talk I talk with a wheeze

My pulse is weak, my blood is thin,
But I'M *AWFULLY WELL* for the state I'm in.

I've got arch supports for both my feet
Without them I couldn't go out in the street
Sleep is denied me night after night
But every morning I find I'm alright
My memory's failing, my head's in a spin
But I'M *AWFULLY WELL* for the state I'm in.

The moral is, as my tale I unfold
That for *You* and *Me* who are both growing old
It's better to say 'I'm fine' with a grin
Than to let other folk know the state we are in
How do I know that my youth is now spent?
Well my GET UP AND GO just got up and WENT.

Old age is golden I've heard it said
But sometimes I wonder as I get into bed
My ears in the drawer, my teeth in a cup
My eyes on the table until I wake up
As sleep overtakes me I say to myself
Is there anything else I should lay on the shelf?

When I was young my slippers were red
I could kick my heels right over my head!
As I grew older my slippers were blue
But still I could dance the whole night through
Now I'm older, my slippers are black
I dash to the shops, but puff my way back.

At last dear Doris my tale is told
So harken you all who are now growing old
Get up each morning, sharpen your wits
Pick up the paper and read the obits

If your name isn't in there, you'll know you're not
dead
So have a good breakfast then go back to bed.

So when you've read this just say with a grin
Old so and so's not too bad
FOR THE STATE HE'S IN!!

Thank you George, I feel a lot better for that!
This next poem *Tribute to a Medium*, brought tears to
my eyes when I read it. It's by Sylvia Mallett.

Tribute To A Medium

There she sat, centre stage, an ordinary woman like
me,
Nothing special about her, well nothing that I could
see.
Why had they come all of these folk, what did they
think she could do?
Why had I come I asked myself when I don't
believe in you.

Too much sorrow had touched my life, too many
tears I'd shed
And now the hardest blow of all, my most dearly
beloved was dead.

I will walk out now I thought, (I must have been
out of my head),
When a voice came floating across the crowd, is
Eileen here, she said.
Bert says to tell you he's OK and why did you cry
today,
When you walked down the garden to his old shed

and threw all his things away.
He was walking with you and felt your gloom and
this made him ever so sad.
Because he is happy and wants you to know that
on this side nothing is bad.
Wait for the flowers to bloom in the Spring, the
ones that you both chose with care,
As they appear and make your heart dance, you'll
know that I am there.

So many messages she gave out that night to
people lost in grief,
So much love poured from her heart as she said
sorry it's been so brief.
She was weary now, but still she tried to pass out
comfort and hope.
Still she smiled that radiant smile as she begged us,
please don't mope.
The door never closes, it's always ajar and you can
step inside.
If you remember with love all those that you've lost
they are always by your side.

An ordinary woman, was that what I'd thought as I
scoffed and made up jokes.
She is no ordinary woman I say, she's special she's
Doris Stokes.

I think I shall pin that poem up on my wall, and
when the critics get me down I'll recite it over and over
again to remind myself what my work's all about.

On a more serious note, Shirley Sutcliffe's poem,
inspired by the death of her mother, sums up the
feelings often experienced by those who see someone
die.

171

Wait! I was to hear her cry,
Not now, please wait a while
I want to see the flowers grow
Not have them when they're there for show
Had I known it would be so soon
I would have listened more in tune.
I didn't know, I couldn't guess
That time would be so much less
Than I had hoped and prayed
No! That's a lie
Perhaps that's why I know you're there
I feel your hand
Not cold but warm like sun kissed sand
I'm ready now lets go in haste
Before I lose this joyous taste.

At that her eyes were still, at peace,
A look of wonder, a smile in crease
I felt no sadness, How could I?
It made one think
Life is given to die.

Shirley's mother had obviously caught sight of her loved ones in the spirit world who had come to meet her, and her passing was so happy that it stopped those who witnessed it in their tracks.

It's surprising how common this is. Even people who've previously scoffed at the idea of life after death have found their views profoundly changed by watching someone 'die'.

And some psychic people are able to sense their own passing months in advance and are able to leave behind words of comfort.

I'm sure this must have been the case with Frank Walsh. He wrote my next poem *Passing Over* two years before his death, and the moving words were read out at his funeral.

Passing Over

Shed no tears when I am leaving,
They won't help me on my way;
Stop the sentimental grieving,
Let it be a normal day.
I am simply passing over,
To a better way of life,
From this testing-ground of living,
Strewn with trouble and with strife.
Help me to prepare with fervour,
My last moments by your side,
So that I may be the stronger,
When I cross the Great Divide.
We will meet in the hereafter,
I don't know exactly when,
There will be much joy and laughter,
But my darling until then —
Know that I am always with you,
Every moment every day;
Waking, sleeping, meditating,
I'll never be far away,
So take heart and be not lonely,
Let me feel your love in prayer,
And remember that I'm only,
Always, ever, waiting there.

No matter how comforting the words however, it's always painful for those of us who're left behind. Even the strongest believers in life after death can't escape grief. It's only natural because even though we know that the separation isn't permanent, we miss the physical presence of our loved one. We need them with us here, we think, and so we grieve. But grief is a healing process. The tears must be shed in order for us to get over the shock and pick up the pieces and start again.

The worst grief I believe comes with the loss of a child and I can hardly read this next poem sent to me by Mrs Jean Bayford without dissolving into tears. But don't be put off by that because it's so beautiful. It sums up everything I hoped for for my little John Michael when he was taken from me at five months old. Unfortunately Jean doesn't say who wrote it. Perhaps it is anonymous.

Farewell To A Little Boy

Honey there will be a hoop
And hill to roll it down ...
(God wouldn't give a little boy the burden of a
    crown)
He'll show you lots of trees to climb
And where he keeps the swings.
(God let him have a bat and ball instead of shining
    wings).
And will he let you sail a kite up where the sky is
    clear
Without tall buildings stooping down?
Of course he will my dear!
Now close your eyes ... I'll kiss them shut
The way I always do. ....
(I must not, *must not* cry dear God I know he's safe
    with you).

Some parents of course are devastated not by the loss of a child, but by the birth of a handicapped child. Andrew Hughes in his poem *Little Did We Know*, which is, I suspect autobiographical, puts this heartache into perspective and points out the joys these children bring with them.

Little Did We Know

Little did we know these few years ago
When we first began our days as man and wife
Little did we know all the heartache we'd go
    through
And the many different views we'd see of life.

We know nothing of immobility, of handicaps or
    spasticity
We thought these things were far away from home
Oh, we'd heard in different places of some isolated
    cases
But we never dreamt we'd have one of our own.

When our daughter was born though in Swindon
    that morning
We knew that she could lose her life
But nothing could compare with the shock and
    despair
As the doctors confronted my wife.

They said she'd not walk, they said she'd not talk
She was blind and would never see
What they failed to impart was what she'd have in
    her heart
And what really good fun she could be.

We don't need sympathy cos we love her you see
And although her needs are really demanding
We'll give her our best, let the future do the rest
All we ask for is some understanding.

We're four now but hey there's another on the way
Should we worry, be frightened or what?
No we'll sit back and trust that our next child will
    just
Be as much fun as the ones that we've got.

If there's a message to say to all parents today
It's this, and I hope you take heed
For life with a spastic can be just as fantastic
Trust in God and that's all you need.

Finally I thought it would be nice to end with a little philosophy. John Pratt's poem *Nothing Comes Easy* is worth repeating aloud in all those impatient, frustrated moments we none of us escape. John was actually writing about his early days in spiritualism but I think his words apply just as well to life in general.

Nothing Comes Easy

Are you searching for something that's so hard to
    find?
In need of a friend, or just peace of mind,
There's an answer to all things, believe me, I know,
But remember that nothing comes easy.

Learning to walk before you can run,
Can take longer than expected I know I was one
Who wanted a miracle, an instant result,

176

But remember that nothing comes easy.

Practice makes perfect the old saying goes.
A man only reaps the seeds that he sows.
Go slowly and surely, absorb what you're told
And remember that nothing comes easy.

It's wrong to see others more learned than you
And envy them for the things they can do,
I'm sure they've been told many times before now
To remember that nothing comes easy.

So remember, whatever it is that you need
It has to be worth waiting for. .... Agreed?
Be patient my friend and keep one thing in mind,
You've been told that nothing comes easy.

Chapter Twelve

Every day, as I've mentioned before, I get dozens and dozens of letters and although most of them contain requests for sittings, this isn't true of them all. Many are what I call my 'tonic letters'. Words of thanks and appreciation that do so much to make me feel that all the hard work is worthwhile. Others are simply accounts of interesting experiences that readers wanted to share with me.

They are such a fascinating and varied mixture that I thought you might like to see a few of them:

Dear Doris,

I have read all of your books and how I would love to meet you and talk to you.

I'm not asking for a sitting, for you help so many people already and you must get so desperately tired at times.

What I wanted to say is, I 'died' thirty years ago and it was an incredibly beautiful experience.

I was almost four months pregnant when I fell downstairs. This shock caused a miscarriage and I lost so much blood that I was admitted to hospital for a D & C. I was in dreadful pain but was told I would only be in the operating theatre for twenty minutes.

The anaesthetist put me out and suddenly I had no more pain. I was so warm it was like being wrapped in soft black velvet. I was holding a flower and was filled with such a deep sense of peace and happiness. At first I floated slowly through the black tunnel towards a light that seemed far away.

Then suddenly, came the LOVE. I was surrounded by it, filled with it, it was everywhere. I knew it was the most perfect and unselfish love and it was taking me faster and faster with it into the beautiful place that I knew was waiting for me in that gloriously brilliant light which grew stronger every moment. I wanted that LOVE, Doris, so very much and the being who was giving it to me, but suddenly I was looking at a clock and feeling not only icy coldness and pain but also utter despair for it had all been snatched away and I was back in the ward. It was two and a half hours after being taken to the theatre. The porters were just putting me back on the bed and the evening visitors were arriving.

Oh Doris to have had it all taken away like that seemed so cruel, even now I have to hold back the tears when I think of it.

I supposed I was sent back because of the children and yet I have the feeling there must have been more that I was meant to do.

When I try to tell people about it they look at me in a way that makes me believe they are very sceptical yet if they would only listen, they would never be afraid of death again. I know that when my time comes I will go gladly and with a prayer of thanks to that being who loved me so completely in spite of all my faults.

My love to you
Mrs H.
Harrogate,
Yorks

I would be very interested to hear of other readers' experiences of 'dying'.

Dear Doris,
   I just had to drop this card to let you know what a laugh it was lining up for tickets this evening.

Of course everyone was saying they felt like a frozen *****s. But stood behind us were a couple of real naturals. They had the crowd in stitches.

They said, 'Well if they don't start selling the tickets soon, Doris won't have an audience — we'll all be over the other side!' You can imagine the laugh.

Thank you for the coffee. We waited for 3½ hours but were lucky to get tickets.

I am glad you love your lovely house. I used to clean it for the next to last owner.

We have lived close by you for twenty-nine years and I could not think of a nicer place to live.

I am on your last book and the photo of you and your hubby in your sitting room I can well imagine because I have cleaned it so many times.

Had to laugh about Freddie Starr wanting to park his helicopter in the garden! He could have landed over on the sports ground by my husband's allotment. What a grand person Freddie is.

I'm not looking for a sitting. I am one of the lucky ones.

Hope your health is keeping well,

Mrs E.H.
London

Dear Mrs Stokes,

I must start off by apologising for the disgusting pen colour [it was bright turquoise!] but I couldn't find anything formal! I am thirteen years old and I have just read all of your excellent books.

I first saw you on telly and from that day I have been a dedicated fan. I hope you write more books as they are so intriguing and I just cannot put them down.

A few days ago we had a discussion on spiritualism, ouija boards, etc. in an RE lesson and I am lucky to have quite an open-minded RE teacher who didn't put down every suggestion of abnormal happenings. In fact I was very suprised and enjoyed the discussion. But near the end I asked him if he had ever heard of Doris Stokes. He then went on to talk about what you did and all that, telling us he'd read *Voices in My Ear* — then he said something that made my blood boil. He said you were a fake.

I went mad! He told us that he thought the spirits giving you information were bad and imitated friends and relatives etc because God condemns contact with the dead.

I told him that the Bible also says to test the spirits to see if they are good — and he sort of mumbled something incomprehensible. I suppose he is entitled to his own opinion but I just had a heart attack.

I have leant my books to friends that asked about you and we have agreed to go to one of your performances if you tour again.

Did you know that you helped me come top of the year in last year's English exam?! You see I had to write a story on 'A figure from the past' — So I wrote about a family who thought their dead baby boy was a figure from the past, but really he was alive and growing by their sides all the time. Now I am very average at most subjects so when I received my paper back I couldn't believe it! If I didn't know what I know from you — I would have come about 99th!!

Forget about Joan Collins and Lady Di — you are my heroine Doris,

Keep going cherub, love to everyone,

lots and lots and lots of love,

Amy,
Sydenham

Dear Doris,

Last night my family and I watched you on Jimmy Young's TV programme. We could tell that you were utterly frustrated and not well yourself, we were so sad about it that I felt I must write and say thank you for all the comfort and hope that you give to so many, many people.

I've bought all your books and found them fascinating so much so that when a young piano pupil lost her little sister I gave them to the family to read. She wrote to you and was overjoyed to receive an answer. The difference you have made to that child is remarkable — and her piano work is now back to normal!

Please don't trouble to reply, I know how much

mail you will receive. Just accept my thanks and best wishes too for a speedy recovery so that you may continue God's work,

Yours
Mrs S.
Leeds

Dear Doris,

Please find enclosed a photograph of my precious little girl Mikaela.

Mikaela was a perfectly healthy little girl until October 25th, 1985 when she contracted a very rare virus called Reyes Syndrome and within 24 hours of her falling ill, she died.

My husband and daughter Kerri are absolutely devastated and feel so lost without her.

I have read all of your books and would be very honoured and grateful if you could put Mikaela's photograph with all the other children on your board. I know she would feel at home there and I would feel a little bit better knowing she was there.

I really hope this letter reaches you. Please look after Mikaela for us too, we love and miss her so much, it's so very hard to go on,

Yours in friendship,
Mrs W.
Cornwall

Dear Doris,

I just wanted to write to you and say 'thank you' for the peace of mind you have brought me. It was quite by chance that a friend at work gave me a copy of *Whispering Voices* to read. I found this so interesting I went out and bought your other books to read.

This year did not start out very well for my husband and myself. We have been married nine years and this September we were both delighted to find I was pregnant for the first time. At first I couldn't believe it, I was so afraid something would happen and we'd find it was a mistake. As time went by I eventually started to let myself start planning for the new baby. In the New Year we decided we'd start looking round for things for the baby.

Then things started to go wrong. I had opted to have the blood test to detect spina bifida, never thinking anything would be wrong. To our dismay it was. I had an amniocentesis and very detailed scans and our baby was diagnosed as having spina bifida and a build up of fluid on the brain. The doctors advised us that our baby could be crippled and may suffer brain damage. We were shattered. We learnt this just before Christmas and really didn't know what to do. The hospital suggested I have another scan in the New Year to see if any more information could be obtained.

Anyway in January and twenty weeks pregnant I had my scan. The diagnosis was confirmed, in fact the fluid in the brain had increased. My husband said he didn't want his child to suffer numerous operations as would probably be the case and perhaps not even then have a good chance of survival. I knew I didn't either but felt that termination still seemed an awful thing.

Anyway after much talking between ourselves with the family and doctors we decided to terminate the pregnancy. My husband was with me the whole time and we saw our daughter afterwards. She was so lovely and perfect looking even at twenty-one weeks apart from her back.

Since then even though I have told myself that it was for the best, still I have felt guilty and like a murderer until I read your books. Particularly in *More Voices in My Ear*, regarding your visit to the spirit world in the last chapter. When I came to the part where you visited the 'waiting area' where babies return before they are born on earth I burst into tears. Not because I was sad, but it made me happy to think our little girl would be there waiting to be born into the spirit world to be loved and looked after.

In reading your books, until then I wondered what would have happened to our baby, how she could have passed over into the spirit world if she had never actually 'lived' here on earth. Now I know it was right to end my pregnancy. Instead of having to have known pain and suffering here on earth in her life, now she will only know love and happiness.

Your books have given me a completely new outlook on life. I always thought there was something else but could never really imagine it. From reading all your experiences and how you have helped so many people, I now believe absolutely in the spiritual side of things and it has seemed to bring so much more hope and love into my life.

Anyway sorry this letter has been so long, I know you get so many, but I really wanted to write and say thank you so much for bringing new hope and happiness into my life at a time when I was feeling pretty awful about things.

With love,
Mrs A.
Chingford

Dear Doris,

I hope this letter finds you in good health. I'm just writing to thank you for the marvellous reading you gave to me and my family when we saw you at the London Palladium. We are all confirmed believers in the after life and have been for quite a while. But what you said, just made us even more sure that we don't die, but live on in another better life with God.

My father died when I was nine years old and my brothers were five and six. Mum had a hard job bringing us up but she was always there when we needed her, with lots of love and cuddles. She's always been the type of mum that we could talk to about anything and of course we were all so very happy for her when she remarried a very kind and caring man.

My dad was only thirty-six when he died but I knew even then that he hadn't really left us. I've always been aware of his presence around us. At night I used to feel the end of my bed go down as if someone had sat there to say 'Goodnight'. And I was never scared, after all it was only Dad. As I got older my interest in the Spiritualist Church and its beliefs grew, as did the interest of the rest of the family.

I've seen my dad a couple of times, not a crystal clear imagine, but all the same I knew it was him. Anyway after our visit to you I wrote an account of our reading. We were so surprised to get something, out of all those people there. But obviously Dad was keen to get through because he even came through on the previous reading. So from all the family, thank you and God bless,

Miss W.
Surrey

Dear Doris,

I lost my dear wife three days before our 43rd wedding anniversary whilst we were on holiday in Jersey.

I can't even begin to tell you the devastating effect this had on me. I was so in love with her. I had been so lucky to marry the prettiest girl in our small mining village where we were both born.

I prayed each time I took flowers to her grave that I could be given a sign that one day we would meet again.

God surely works in a mysterious way. One Sunday morning I went to the local newsagent to get my usual Sunday paper. They had sold out but the paper I did get showed on its book page the publication of *Whispering Voices*.

I had heard of you but I must admit only vaguely. I certainly didn't know that you had written any books. I read quite a lot.

I have now read all five.

I am so grateful to you for the comfort they have given me and to know that I shall meet my dearest wife again.

God bless you Doris and John too. I shall be ever grateful.

Mr T.
Wales

Dear Doris,

I am writing to say thank you for the relief I feel, having read your wonderful books. I no longer cry over my stillborn baby as much as I used to.

I still feel after ten years I would like to have seen her and held her for just a moment and in my circumstances, unmarried and penniless, I agreed for the hospital to make the funeral arrangements. It wasn't until I got home to my parents' house that the overwhelming grief really hit me.

I phoned the hospital to find out where she was either buried or cremated, but they didn't know. I was given the name of the funeral parlour but they didn't have a record of a baby girl so I was at a dead end. My Natalie Amy had just gone and I didn't know where.

Now dear Doris after ten years I know she is with all the other spirit children, with my two miscarried brothers and your own dear son John Michael.

Doris I have cried with you and laughed with you. Because of you I am now looking forward with happiness, not fear for my time to go over to come, so I may hold my Natalie Amy in my arms at last. But first I want to see my son grow and marry and even make us grandparents, but he's only four now so I am going to give him as much as I can before we come to that stage.

I have a lot to do before then and I want to make as much out of my life as I can.

Well we've made ourselves members of your Sod-It Club. When we feel nothing is going right anymore we think of what you say, and we say Sod It! and it all goes better after that. My son has even joined in, when his puzzles don't go right or he's not near enough to the loo and misses he says 'Mummy's sod it!'

Thanks to you for being a friend to us and millions like us,

May God bless you and yours
Mrs S.
Canterbury

Chapter Thirteen

I think it was the day the car came through our front garden wall that did it. There we were, minding our own business one Saturday morning, when suddenly there was a great screech of tyres across the road, followed by a tremendous bang.

Horrified, we ran outside to see an ancient and now much battered Triumph Herald in the garden and a gaping hole in the front wall six feet above it, (our house is set down from the road, consequently our garden is several feet below the pavement).

Shocked, I dashed inside to call an ambulance, but fortunately the driver wasn't hurt.

What a day we had. Police, ambulancemen, garage people to remove the car, builders to make the wall safe — it was like Piccadilly Circus and the kitchen was turned into a mini cafe to cope with all the cups of tea.

The driver must have been a bit dazed because all he could think about was his car.

'When will my car be back on the road?' he kept asking anyone who'd listen.

One of the policemen eyed the wreck with distaste. Even before its argument with our brick wall it was clear that the only thing holding the car together was the rust.

'Never,' he said grimly. 'And have you got an MOT for that?'

But the aftermath of the accident was only phase I. Phase II was the rebuilding of the wall, a long and complicated job because the entire wall had to be removed and rebuilt with special reinforcing. There seemed to be no end to it.

For a long time I'd been feeling in need of a break but now it came to a head. If I didn't get away for some peace and quiet, I'd go mad I told myself.

It's funny, I always used to think that if you lived in a nice place you wouldn't need to go away for a holiday. A deckchair in the garden'll be good enough for me when I get my house I used to say, but now I've got it, I find that that's not true. Working from home means that you can never really stop working while you're there. You can't stop the phone ringing or the mail from dropping through the letter box, and despite your good intentions you soon find yourself being drawn back onto the merry-go-round.

It soon became obvious that a holiday was essential, but where? I'm lucky enough to have dozens of invitations to all sorts of exotic places. The other day someone even invited me to stay with them in Istanbul! But quite honestly I do so much travelling throughout the year, the last thing I want to do with my time off is climb on a plane. Neither do I want to stay in hotels. I see enough hotel rooms when I'm working to last me a life time, nice though most of them are.

Another problem about staying in public places is that these days people tend to recognise me and many of them don't seem to understand that when I'm on holiday I need to rest.

'I know you're very, very busy,' they say, 'but couldn't you just do a sitting for me?'

It's very difficult to say 'no' and sometimes I'd rather stay in my room than risk meeting someone like this.

The problem was still unresolved when one day I picked up the local paper and saw the solution staring me in the face. There was an advert for a number of holiday cottages for sale on a site near the coast. Apparently a former holiday camp had been taken over and the new owners were renovating the old chalets and selling them privately.

I'd never heard of the place so I asked Terry, who does a lot of driving about, where it was.

'Only about forty-five minutes from here in the car,' he said.

'That'll do me,' I said happily.

It was the ideal answer. Since the chalets were being sold privately the same people would use them all the time and if they recognised me, they'd soon get used to me and realise I didn't want to work on holiday. What's more, the place was close enough to keep travelling to a minimum, yet near enough to the sea to be a real tonic.

'Oh Terry, let's take a run over there and look at it!' I said.

So one bleak, windswept day we drove down to the chalet park. It was only five minutes' walk from the sea and the fresh, ozone smell caught in my throat as soon as I stepped out of the car. The site was open with a big grassy space in the middle and a number of neat little chalets around the edge.

We were shown to a semi-detached cottage near the park boundary. The decorating wasn't finished but you could see the place was going to be nice. There was a good sized living room with a fitted kitchen leading off it through an archway, and at the other side of the room, doors opened into two airy bedrooms and a modern bathroom. Outside there was a tiny lawn overlooking a little stream. What's more, the site contained an indoor swimming pool, and a takeaway restaurant in case you didn't feel like cooking.

It was ideal.

'We'll take it!' I said.

The people who run the park were marvellous. I was too busy to get down to the cottage to organise the furnishing and colour schemes, so the wife of the owner did it for me. And what a wonderful job she did. The sitting room was all in shades of pale green, the main bedroom pink, the kitchen beige and the bathroom, deep sea green. It was beautiful.

Our first week's holiday wasn't without its teething troubles however. Terry brought us down one Friday morning for a snatched week in the spring between theatre bookings. Everything was wonderful. John and I spent a happy afternoon unpacking and admiring the beautiful rooms. We weren't planning to do anything. I'd brought a stack of books and I was looking forward to peace, quiet, a good read and watching the seagulls drift by.

But Saturday didn't turn out quite as planned.

Everything went well until lunch time when without warning the electricity went off. The cottage was all electric so very soon we were shivering and we couldn't so much as make a cup of tea. All the other cottages in our part of the park were similarly affected, but undaunted, the family who ran the place raced up and down ferrying boiling kettles of water from cottage to cottage from their own house which still had electricity.

It was funny to watch all those hurrying kettles and the curious gliding run with which they were carried so as not to spill a drop, but after a while it got beyond a joke. Hours passed and there was still not a spark of electricity in the cottage.

John and I were frozen and we wondered if we should go home.

'This holiday won't do us much good if we both catch pneumonia,' I said. 'But if we go now I won't feel like coming back later in the week. I don't think I could face all that packing and unpacking twice.'

Terry offered to come and fetch us, but still we dithered. And it's just as well we did.

At five o'clock the owners took pity on us and invited us to sit by the fire in their house and there we stayed until 11.45, when the electricity finally came back on!

Well it was certainly an experience, and I must say I've never drunk so many cups of tea in my life!

I'm very glad we stayed. The weather was gloomy but it didn't matter. The air was very strong and we slept like logs and by the end of the week I felt much more refreshed.

But we did have a bit of excitement. While we were at the cottage, John Inman from *Are You Being Served,* came to tea.

I adore John Inman as a comic. Most years Terry gives me theatre tickets to a good show for my birthday and once he managed to get me into *Mother Goose* with John Inman. Unknown to me, Terry had phoned John's manager and asked if John could wish me happy birthday from the stage.

Well I knew nothing about it and there I was watching the show and laughing my head off when John suddenly said, 'Oh I see the Duchess is here.' (Terry

always calls me the Duchess, I don't know why.)
'Happy Birthday Doris,' John went on, 'and what
would you like for your birthday?'

'You John!' I said. 'Are you free?'

'I'm free!' he said. 'And have you anything to tell
me?'

'Yes, everything's going to be all right.'

'Thank goodness,' he said.

And that was my only encounter with John Inman,
or so I thought. But then *Psychic News* phoned me as
they do every year to see if I could get any of my show
business friends to be guest of honour at the annual
dinner dance, and make a funny speech.

Well I tried Freddie Starr, but he was working that
day and I didn't know what to do.

'Can you think of anyone, Fay?' I asked Fay Hillier
when she phoned one day. Fay was the girlfriend of
my old friend Dick Emery. I'd met her through Dick
and I'd been able to give her a few personal details in a
sitting after he passed, which seemed to impress her
and we've been close ever since.

'Well I'm appearing in a play with John Inman at the
moment,' she said, 'I could ask him.'

To my delight, because I love John Inman, he agreed
but he wanted to meet me first and hear more about
Psychic News and what he would have to do.

'I'll bring him down to the cottage,' said Fay. 'He'll
love it.'

So the Thursday of the visit we were bustling round
polishing everything that stood still until the whole
place sparkled. By an amazing stroke of luck, the
daughter of the family which runs the site is a caterer
and she offered to make some dainty sandwiches for
me. But hours before John was due to arrive she staggered in with the most fantastic buffet you've ever

seen. It was like the cold table at a wedding reception.

'Well if this doesn't impress them nothing will,' I said, as she laid it all out on the table and around the kitchen. 'You've gone mad, Kathy.'

Our visitors arrived just after 4.00. Fay, who's an ex-bluebell girl with legs that go on for ever, was wearing an off-white leather jacket, off-white boots and a pair of off-white pants with green stripes.

'She looks like a tube of toothpaste!' said John Inman.

John himself was conservatively dressed in a navy blue blazer and slacks, with a trilby complete with feather to top it off.

He looked just the same as he does on TV, but he's not at all camp and unlike his TV personality, he's a very shy boy. At one point Kathy put her head round the door and asked if her little daughter could just come and have a peep at John Inman. The child was only a schoolgirl, but John was so shy he blushed.

Like so many big stars he wasn't at all grand. I didn't have to fuss round him. He made himself at home and soon he was wandering round the kitchen supervising the tea-making because: 'I do like a good cup of tea.'

Generally he was quiet and fairly serious but when he told us his funny stories he had us in stitches.

'Shall I tell you how I first met Fay?' he asked. 'Well I was in New Zealand waiting for a plane to Australia and I had about three hours to wait.

'The man who was looking after me suggested I go and sit by the pool in a nice hotel nearby and he said he'd pick me up later in plenty of time for the flight. So I was sitting there on a sunlounger having a drink when all of a sudden I noticed this creature coming towards me. He was wearing a safari suit and dark glasses and he was mincing along the pool.

'My God, I thought, that creature is coming straight for me. And he was. "Hello Ducky," he said when he got to my sunbed, "are you lonely?"

'I was just going to tell him where to go when he suddenly started to laugh. It was Dick Emery. He had the most infectious laugh you ever heard.

'Apparently he'd been sitting on the other side of the pool with Fay and he said, "Won't be a minute, I've just spotted someone I know," and he put on his camp act and came mincing over. Of course he introduced me to Fay then and we've been friends ever since.'

It turned out that John had also been a friend of Diana Dors and we swopped stories about that lovely lady. John too had been impressed with her courage and kindness. Even Fay had reason to be grateful to her.

Apparently while Dick was seriously ill in hospital, Fay was marooned at his bedside, unable to pop out for meals because the press were hounding her. When Diana, also a friend of Dick's, got to hear about it, she had sandwiches sent in to Fay every day and arranged for a car to take her to and from the hospital.

All in all it was a very enjoyable afternoon and we were sorry to see them go when they left for the journey back to London at 8.00.

There was another enjoyable interlude around this time. About two months before, I'd been invited to a function at the Institute for the Blind in which a new machine called a moon writer was presented.

Apparently it was invented by three schoolboys and their science teacher, and it is a godsend for the blind.

The machine is like a typewriter but it produces big raised letters on the paper so that a blind person can read the letter by touch without having to learn braille.

196

The machine can also produce raised letters on strips of metal to be attached to tins and cartons of food so that a blind person can go through his store cupboard and choose exactly what he wants to eat without fear of opening a tin of peaches instead of a tin of salmon.

I thought it was a marvellous idea and I enthused about it to the other guests, most of them authors whose books had been translated into braille. There was Molly Weir, Hammond Innes, John Le Carre and many others. Wouldn't it be wonderful if one day, every blind person in the country had their own moonwriter and learned how to use it, I thought. It could make such a difference to their lives.

'If I buy five for them, will you buy five?' I asked Sue Townsend, the author of the Adrian Mole books.

'Certainly,' said Sue.

So it was arranged. I don't know what Sue did with hers but a few weeks later I went to Linden Lodge, a special school in Wimbledon, to make my own presentation.

Linden Lodge was an inspiring place. A large old house at the end of a long drive, it was surrounded by the most beautiful gardens. Lawns sloped away to a tennis court, and there were sweetly scented flowers and great leafy trees all over the place. In the courtyard three rabbits frisked around on a patch of grass and a silky cat watched them without interest. They were quite safe with her.

Inside the house was comfortable and well laid out. We were led from classroom to recreation room and even, I was amazed to see, a fully equipped gymnasium where blind children leapt about fearlessly. Watching them jump and run without a second's hesitation, you'd never have guessed these children couldn't see.

Finally we came to the classroom where the presentation was to take place. The children waited patiently at their little tables, quiet and well-behaved although they must have been getting very bored. We were so interested in everything we were shown at Linden Lodge that we had taken far longer than expected to reach the classroom.

It wouldn't have been right to make a speech to these little mites, so I just wished them lots of fun with their new machines and presented the moonwriter to a slender little black boy. He took it back to his table and immediately most of the children clustered round to finger it wonderingly.

One little girl named Carol gravitated towards me however.

'Can I talk to you?' she asked. 'You smell like my mummy and I do miss my mummy.'

Poor little soul, I thought. It must be bad enough to be blind without having to be parted from your mother as well, even though it was for her own good.

'Yes you come and sit here, love,' I told her. 'But don't forget it's Friday tomorrow so you'll be going home.'

Her face lit up. 'Is it Friday tomorrow? Oh good.'

She chatted to me for a while then she asked, 'Can I feel your necklace?'

'Of course you can,' I told her and I bent down while her small fingers explored my necklace, my neck and then on to my face.

They were lovely children, calm, polite and obedient, yet some of them had been difficult when they first arrived, the teacher told us. There was one little boy in particular who had been uncontrollable when he came to the school a year before. He used to shout all the time at the top of his voice. Then they discovered he was deaf as well as blind but nobody had realised it until then and the poor lad was simply trying to make his presence known in the only way he could.

He was fitted with a special hearing aid and now he sits as quietly as the other children listening to the lessons.

By this time the teacher had become very interested in the moonwriter and he took out the instruction leaflet to find out how to operate it. The children became restless and out of the corner of my eye I noticed a pile of rolled-up towels on a table at the back of the room.

'Are you going swimming?' I asked the teacher.

'Yes,' he said glancing up from the instructions. 'When we've finished here they're going swimming.'

There was something about the expectant, impatient look in the children's faces that made me feel we were outstaying our welcome.

'I think we'd better leave, Laurie,' I said quietly. 'The kids are waiting to go swimming.'

But I'd forgotten the acute hearing of the blind and one of the girls caught my words.

'We don't want to appear rude and ask you to go,' she said earnestly, 'but we do want to go swimming.'

I thought that was hilarious. 'That's right, dear, you tell us to go,' I said patting her cheek and trying to keep the laughter out of my voice. 'Of course you want to go swimming.'

We said our goodbyes, and polite as ever, the children gathered gravely round to thank us for coming.

Returning home from Linden Lodge was just like coming back from a refreshing holiday. The presence of children always has a tonic effect on me. In their company I forget all my problems and worries, all my aches and pains fade away and I enter their innocent world.

These days I get asked to do all kinds of exciting things. I mentioned earlier about being approached to switch on the Christmas lights in Halifax. Well, not long ago I achieved another ambition — I opened a fete. The story started in fact some months before. Earlier in the year after our long, terrible winter I was feeling in need of a holiday. It was still so wet and cold that someone suggested John and I go on a cruise.

'It's expensive,' they warned, 'but it's so relaxing. You really unwind. It's worth every penny.'

They were so enthusiastic that by the end of the conversation John and I were convinced that a cruise was the only thing that would set us up for the rest of the year.

'I'll go down to the travel agents on Monday,' John said, 'and book us up.'

There was a gap in my bookings coming up and we were hoping to leave on the next available boat, so I started sorting through my wardrobe putting to one side the things I would take.

'We're going on a cruise!' I told everyone proudly.

And so we were. But then the next morning I opened the paper and read a particularly tragic story. A young mother had lost her unborn baby because her local hospital in Basildon didn't have enough foetal heart monitors. Apparently these machines can detect if anything is going wrong with the child, and if so the medical team can step in. Perhaps the baby would have passed over anyway, who knows, but the distressed girl was convinced that a monitor could have saved her child's life.

Having lost three unborn babies myself, I knew how

she felt. If there had been a machine available in my day which might have saved my children's life I would have wanted heaven and earth moved to provide it for them.

Impulsively I phoned the newspaper and asked how much the monitors cost. The price turned out to be near enough what we'd planned to spend on the cruise.

'All right, tell the hospital I'll buy them one,' I said to the astonished reporter.

As I put the phone down I turned round and saw that John had come quietly into the room and was grinning at me.

'Oh John, I'm sorry,' I said. 'You didn't really want to go on the cruise did you? It's much better to save all those babies.'

'Of course it is, love. I don't really mind. There's always next year.'

The hospital wrote a beautiful thank you letter and that I thought was the end of the matter until a few months later they contacted me again. They were organising a summer fete to raise more funds and they wondered if I'd like to officially open it. While I was there perhaps I'd like to see the monitor I'd bought and have a conducted tour of the baby unit?

It sounded to me a lovely way to spend an afternoon and I accepted gladly. A few weeks later John, Laurie, Jean, who helps me with my cleaning, and I piled into the car on a hot, sunny morning and made our way to Basildon.

'There's going to be a baby born while we're there,' I said suddenly as we sped along. 'I'd better buy it a present.'

'You've been talking to them upstairs again,' said Laurie.

And I had to smile. I knew I was right because I'd heard a spirit voice say, 'The baby won't be long now. He'll be born while you're there.'

I'd not been to Basildon before and it struck me as an impressive place: spacious and new with wide airy streets and bright flower beds.

Our first stop was the hospital building itself and Laurie found it without difficulty. Outside was gathered a little welcoming committee headed by chairman Tom Swan, and after the introductions we were whisked away to maternity to inspect the first baby unit. There in pride of place stood our heart monitor, complete with a little plaque which read: 'Presented by spiritualist Doris Stokes.' But it was also covered by a cloth.

'I wouldn't let anyone use it until you'd been,' said the sister, who'd actually come in on her holiday to watch me officially hand over the machine. She removed the cloth and I looked at the monitor with interest. It was rather like an ordinary heart machine with a print-out for the heart-beats, but it didn't mean a lot to me. Things have changed so much since I was a nurse.

'We've got a mother on a monitor now,' said sister, reading my thoughts. 'Would you like to see it working? She doesn't mind.'

The young mother was lying on a bed with sensors on her tummy and the machine by her side. It was quite extraordinary. The monitor picked up the sounds of the baby's heart-beat and magnified it right round the room. Boom — boom — boom — boom went the baby's heart, clearly strong and healthy.

I shook hands with the mother, then I bent down to her tummy and said, 'Are you all right in there?'

And to my amazement the noise changed, speeded

up, and the heart went 'Boomboom boom boom boom.'

'You've got it excited now,' sister laughed.

'I'm sure it knows you're talking to it,' said the mother.

We chatted for a few minutes. She told me she'd got another three weeks to go and confessed that she was a bit frightened of the birth.

'Well it's no picnic, love,' I said, 'but when they lay your baby in your arms you forget all that. I'm sixty-seven and I still remember that wonderful moment when they laid my baby boy in my arms. It was the most wonderful moment of my life.'

Sister was keen to show us the rest of the maternity unit but just as we were leaving the mother and monitor, a thought struck me and I turned back.

'Will you do something for me?' I asked. 'If it's a girl will you call her Charity for her second name, because that means love.'

'Oh yes I will, Doris,' said the mother.

Back outside we toured the maternity ward where I stopped to admire a beautiful baby with the most gorgeous blue eyes. I put my finger down to him and his little fist curled round it and hung on with an amazing grip. Then we went to the special baby unit and stared in astonishment at these tiny little scraps in incubators. The babies were so small you felt you could lay them in the palm of your hand.

From there we went to intensive care where little Philippa, who was having trouble breathing, was on a ventilator.

'But she's doing extremely well now,' said sister.

By now time was getting on and although I could have spent all day with the babies I knew I had to go and open the fete. We retraced our steps and outside the maternity ward we found a young man sitting tensely on a bench.

'He's waiting for his wife to be delivered,' said sister.

'The baby will be born soon love, don't worry,' I told him.

He shrugged, his face pale. 'Oh I don't know. You never can tell,' he said.

I smiled to myself. The spirit world can, I thought, but I didn't say anything. Afterwards they told me he thought I was the mayor!

An hour or so later as I was going round the fete there came an announcement over the loudspeaker.

'Doris Stokes, the baby was born at ten past two, his name's Christopher and he weighs 6lbs.'

'You can always rely on the spirit world,' I told Laurie as I bought the biggest teddy bear I could find for little Christopher.

They had gone to a great deal of trouble with the fete. The field was bright with flags and bunting and the platform was decorated with flowers. There were seventy stalls, a giant rubber castle for the kids to jump on and the local Blue Eagles Band marched up and down playing rousing tunes. Unfortunately the sun had disappeared behind a bank of cloud and a bitter wind sprang up, but the people were determined to have a good time.

'It gives me great pleasure to open this fete,' I said from the platform, 'because I am speaking from both sides of the fence. I've lost four babies and also I'm an ex-nurse. I know what it's like for a mother to lose a baby and also what it's like to be a nurse. When a nurse loses a patient she goes off and has a cry in the bathroom...'

Once the fete was well and truly open we walked

round looking at the stalls and as well as the teddy bear for Christopher I bought a big doll all dressed in pink with frilly underwear, for the first girl born after the visit.

Throughout the afternoon I was kept busy signing autographs, and a number of people came up to thank me for buying the monitor. One lady was particularly moving.

'Can I give you a hug,' said the young mother leading a small girl by the hand. 'I had two miscarriages before I had my little girl and if there'd been a monitor then I might not have lost them. Thank you so much.'

And I thought, 'What's a cruise, if you can do this?'

By now I'd been on my feet for hours it seemed, but there was still one more task to perform. I presented the Vic Mason memorial shield for the St John's Ambulance stretcher race, and then I was able to escape for a quick peep at baby Christopher before I left.

He'd been in this world just two hours when I saw him and his little face was still red, but he was gorgeous. Perfect in every minute detail.

'How can anyone not believe in God?' I wondered, as I stared down at him. 'Surely every new-born baby is a miracle.'

'Never again, never again!' the mother was groaning ruefully but her eyes were alight with joy.

It was a wonderful end to a wonderful day.

'Who cares about a cruise,' I said to Laurie later as we climbed thankfully back into the car. 'I expect I'd have been seasick anyway!'

I enjoy my work, even though it sometimes gets me down, but if in doing my work I can help little children like these, then my pleasure is doubled. Children are our future and we should guard them well.

At the moment strangers coming to my house think I must have a whole family of little ones staying there. There's a rag doll, a teddy bear and a Wurzel Gummidge scarecrow on the sofa, and the mantelpiece is crammed with children's pictures. In fact the toys, like the photographs, belong to children who've recently passed to the spirit world and whose parents want me to keep an eye on them.

The same goes for my board of spirit children which hangs out in the hall where it is the first thing that greets a visitor's eye.

The other day a telephone engineer came to the house to do some work on our phone.

'I'm intrigued by all these pictures of children,' he said, after passing the board for the umpteenth time and staring at it fixedly.

'They're my grandchildren,' I told him.

'Grandchildren?' he said. 'There must be 300 of them. Surely you can't have 300 grandchildren.'

'Well not exactly,' I said. This was going to be difficult. 'They're my spirit grandchildren. They are children who have passed over to the spirit world who have adopted me as their granny because I've brought them back to their parents. After the sittings their parents give me a picture for my wall and the kids can come and see me whenever they want.'

The young man's eyes bulged at that and he backed away rather warily I felt.

'I've just got to go and collect some more equipment,' he said quickly and the next thing I knew he was hurrying outside to his car as if he feared I might pin *him* to my board.

I shrugged to myself and went back to my letters. It's very awkward when people ask you a question but don't really want to hear a truthful answer.

But later on that afternoon the young man re-appeared and his attitude had changed completely.

'All the girls in the office know you,' he told me eagerly, 'and they want to know if I could take your autograph back to prove that I've been here.'

I burst out laughing.

'Of course you can, love,' I said, and I scribbled out my name on a piece of paper for him.

This sort of thing tickles me to death because after all, I'm just an ordinary housewife like thousands of other housewives, struggling to cope with a job and a family, and not always succeeding.

Right now though, fingers and toes crossed, everything seems to be going smoothly. John is pleased because his healing work is going well and he's just had a postcard from a woman who suffered from agrophobia and had not been outside her front door for seven years. She wanted him to know that she was enjoying her first holiday for years thanks to his healing. It made John's day.

I'm pleased because I had a demonstration last week that went particularly well and a TV director in the audience said he'd like to make a film about me.

Of course the chances are it won't come to anything, but you never know. Life is getting so exciting these days I just can't imagine what will happen next!

All Futura Books are available at your bookshop or
newsagent, or can be ordered from the following address:
Futura Books,Cash Sales Department,
P.O. Box 11, Falmouth, Cornwall.

Please send cheque or postal order (no currency), and
allow 55p for postage and packing for the first book
plus 22p for the second book and 14p for each additional
book ordered up to a maximum charge of £1.75 in U.K.

Customers in Eire and B.F.P.O. please allow 55p for
the first book, 22p for the second book plus 14p per
copy for the next 7 books, thereafter 8p per book.

Overseas customers please allow £1 for postage and
packing for the first book and 25p per copy for each
additional book.